SAARINEN HOUSE AND GARDEN

A TOTAL WORK OF ART

SAARINEN HOUSE AND GARDEN

A TOTAL WORK OF ART

GREGORY WITTKOPP, EDITOR

INTRODUCTION BY ROY SLADE

ESSAYS BY GREGORY WITTKOPP AND DIANA BALMORI

COLOR PHOTOGRAPHY BY BALTHAZAR KORAB

HARRY N. ABRAMS, INC., PUBLISHERS, IN ASSOCIATION WITH CRANBROOK ACADEMY OF ART MUSEUM

Project Manager: Margaret L. Kaplan

Editor: Diana Murphy

Designer: Scott W. Santoro • WORKSIGHT

Library of Congress Cataloging-in-Publication Data

Saarinen House and garden: a total work of art/
Gregory Wittkopp, editor; introduction by Roy Slade;
essays by Gregory Wittkopp and Diana Balmori;
color photography by Balthazar Korab.

     p.   cm.

  Includes bibliographical references and index.

  ISBN 0-8109-4462-6

1. Saarinen House (Bloomfield Hills, Mich.)

2. Saarinen, Eliel, 1873–1950–Criticism and interpretation.

3. Saarinen, Eliel, 1873–1950–Homes and haunts–
   Michigan–Bloomfield Hills.

4. Architecture, Domestic–Michigan–Bloomfield Hills–
   Conservation and restoration.

5. Cranbrook Academy of Art.

6. Saarinen House Garden (Bloomfield Hills, Mich.)

7. Bloomfield Hills (Mich.)–Buildings, structures, etc. I. Wittkopp, Gregory.

NA737.S3A53 1995

728'.37'092–dc20   94-33282

                      CIP

Printed and bound in Japan

Frontispiece: Studio Alcove, view from Living Room (plate 77)

*The color photographs of Saarinen House and garden were
taken between September 1993 and June 1994.*

CONTENTS

ACKNOWLEDGMENTS

The restoration of Saarinen House, its transformation into a museum, and the publication of this book was an undertaking that involved many people. In addition to my collaborators on the book—Diana Balmori, Patricia Crow, Balthazar Korab, David D. J. Rau, and Roy Slade—and the many artists, donors, and lenders credited in the catalogue of the Saarinen House Collection, I would like to thank a number of people who played a critical role in this project.

First of all, I would like to extend my profound gratitude to the members of the Saarinen Swanson family—in particular Robert Saarinen Swanson and Ronald Saarinen Swanson—for their generous support of the restoration. Along with their parents, Pipsan Saarinen Swanson and J. Robert F. Swanson, they helped to preserve the cultural heritage of their grandparents' home, finally entrusting it to us at Cranbrook.

Within the Cranbrook Educational Community I would like to thank Lillian Bauder, President, Cranbrook Educational Community, for her commitment to preserving the work of Eliel and Loja Saarinen at Cranbrook. In addition, I would like to thank Mark Coir, Director, Cranbrook Archives and Cultural Properties; Judy Dyki, Librarian, Cranbrook Academy of Art Library; and Karen Serota, Registrar, Cultural Properties; as well as Alan Beeman, Barbara Moon Boertzel, Maureen Brady, Maris Cannon, Gary Griffin, Gerhardt Knodel, Mary Beth Kreiner, Corajoyce Rauss, John Rothfuss, Calvin Sanders, Helga Siner, Richard Smith, and former employees Linnea Aukee, Ralph Mize, and Carolyn Texley. I would like to offer a special thank you to three former curators at Cranbrook Academy of Art Museum—John Gerard, Mary Riordan, and Susan Waller; their efforts helped launch this project. I also want to thank our Saarinen House docents for enthusiastically sharing the restored house with the public as well as the many students—in particular, Christina Bechstein, Paula Stebbins Becker, and Celeste Brush—who worked with me on the restoration. In addition, I would like to acknowledge and thank the past and present members of the Board of Governors of Cranbrook Academy of Art, in particular former Chairpersons Pat Hartmann and Ernie Jones, for their enthusiastic support of the restoration.

For the restoration itself, I am indebted to the skillful work and attention to detail of many people, most notably Lawrence McLoskey and George Stamplis, A Notch Above, Madison Heights, Michigan; William Adair, Gold Leaf Studios, Washington, D.C.; Marvin Niebauer, Rochester Tree and Landscape Company, Oakland, Michigan; and Frank S. Welsh, Historic Paint Color Consultant, Bryn Mawr, Pennsylvania.

A special thank you is due to several individuals at the textile mills that designed, produced, and generously donated fabrics used in the restoration, including Bill Bumstead and Maja Page, Bentley Mills, City of Industry, California; Robert Blum, Jack Eger, and Bruce Shawlis, Craftex Mills, Inc. of Penna., Blue Bell, Pennsylvania; Sam Friedman and Suzanne Tick, Unika Vaev USA/International Contract Furnishings,

New York City; Mark Grigalunas and Henry A. Truslow, Sunbury Textile Mills, Sunbury, Pennsylvania; Liza Lamb, Robert Smart, and Christine Walsh, Collins and Aikman, Bloomfield Hills, Michigan; and Wayne B. Lyon, Masco Corporation, Taylor, Michigan. I also want to thank Charles A. Soberman and the Mercury Paint Company, Detroit, for generously formulating and donating all of the paint used in the restoration. In addition, Bill Greenwood and the Globe Dye Works Company, Philadelphia, kindly dyed and donated yarns used to reweave many of the textiles.

For their guidance and editorial expertise, I want to thank Margaret Kaplan and Diana Murphy at Harry N. Abrams, Inc. I am also delighted that Scott W. Santoro, a graduate of Cranbrook's Design Department, had the opportunity to work with them to realize the book's design.

We received assistance in myriad ways from many colleagues and friends in the United States, including Alfred Ackerman, Carol Forsythe, Barbara Heller, David Penney, and MaryAnn Wilkinson, Detroit Institute of Arts; Sandra Ahlers, formerly of Birmingham, Michigan; Melanie Bazil, Pewabic Pottery, Detroit; John Bowditch, Henry Ford Museum and Greenfield Village, Dearborn, Michigan; Walter Scott Braznell, New Haven, Connecticut; Irving Burton, Huntington Woods, Michigan; Thomas Brunk, Detroit; Margaret B. Caldwell, New York City; Frank T. Coe, Scalamandré, Long Island City, New York; Paul R. Czubay, Textile Conservation, Rochester, New York; Anna Danielson, Waterford, Michigan; Dennis Denomme, Jalil Farah, and Borris Sellers, William Beaumont Hospital, Royal Oak, Michigan; Martin Eidelberg, Rutgers University, New Brunswick, New Jersey; Carolyn Fenningdorf, Lake Orion, Michigan; Barbara Gentile, Leo, Indiana; Ann Gheorghiade, Chicago; Matthew Ginal, Buffalo, New York; Phebe Goldstein, Bloomfield Hills, Michigan; Marianne Strengell Hammarstrom, Wellfleet, Massachusetts; E. Jan Hartmann, Bloomfield Hills, Michigan; Donald Jenkins, Portland Art Museum, Oregon; Kersten Berglund Kavanagh, Iverness, Florida; Terrance Keenan, Syracuse University Library, New York; James Kelly and Mariam Noland, Grosse Pointe Farms, Michigan; Ann Kerr, Sidney, Ohio; Margueritte Kimball, Cambridge, Massachusetts; Douglas Lengyel and Carol Ann Strahl, Kleinhans Music Hall, Buffalo; Brian Madigan, Wayne State University; Russ May, Clarkston, Michigan; David Revere McFadden and Joanne Warner, Cooper–Hewitt National Museum of Design, New York City; Bernice C. Morehouse, Meriden Historical Society, Connecticut; Craig Morrison, Philadelphia; Albert Nesle, Nesle Inc., New York City; Thomas C. Newcomb, Bradbury and Bradbury Art Wallpapers, Benicia, California; Addrienne O'Brien, Matthaei Botanical Gardens, Ann Arbor, Michigan; Derek E. Ostergard, The Bard Graduate Center for Studies in the Decorative Arts, New York City; Glen Paulsen, Ann Arbor; Jessica G. Randolph, Museum of American Textile History, North Andover, Massachusetts; Louis Redstone, Detroit; James Robinson, James Robinson and Associates, Ashburnham, Massachusetts; Carl Rundell, Birmingham, Michigan; Viktor Schreckengost, Cleveland, Ohio; Patricia

Shaw, West Bloomfield, Michigan; Jewel Stern, Coral Gables, Florida; Betty Trost, Birmingham, Michigan; Horst Uhr, Wayne State University; Kathleen Walsh, Nessen Lighting, New York City; Vic West, formerly of Mercury Paint Company, Detroit; and Katherine Zikakis, Birmingham, Michigan.

We received assistance from additional colleagues and friends in Canada and Europe, including Anna-Lisa Amberg and Jarno Peltonen, Museum of Applied Arts, Helsinki, Finland; Bengt von Bonsdorff, Amos Anderson Art Museum, Helsinki; Meredith Chilton, The George R. Gardiner Museum of Ceramic Art, Toronto, Canada; Anita Ehrnrooth, Hvitträsk, Luoma Boback, Finland; Christian Hoffmann, Turku Art Museum, Turku, Finland; Sabine Kulovits, Vienna; Brian Musselwhite, Royal Ontario Museum, Toronto; Riita Nikula and Marja-Riita Norri, Museum of Finnish Architecture, Helsinki; Juhani Pallasmaa, Helsinki; Antti Parkkinen, Helsinki; Heidi Pfäffli, Wäinö Aaltonen Museum, Turku; Maritta Pitkänen, The Gösta Serlachius Museum of Fine Arts, Mänttä, Finland; Elisabeth Schmuttermeier, Austrian Museum for Applied Arts, Vienna; Hanna Kaisa Soini, Helsinki; Alexander Tzonis, University of Technology at Delft, the Netherlands; and Sirkka Valanto, Finnish National Gallery.

I would like to extend a very special thank you to Dora Apel, my wife, and Thomas Trombley, my friend and colleague, whose advice, assistance, encouragement, and support I relied upon from the beginning to the end. Dora's critical mind helped propel me through the research and writing of the book, while Tom's critical eye and sensitivity to architectural practices and techniques helped insure the success of the restoration.

Finally, I would like to offer a sincere thank you to Roy Slade, without whom the restoration of Saarinen House would not have been realized. It was his vision that recognized the genius of Eliel and Loja Saarinen in Saarinen House and his passion for Cranbrook that inspired every step of this project.

Gregory Wittkopp

Director

Cranbrook Academy of Art Museum

INTRODUCTION

Roy Slade

Having accepted the invitation to be the fifth president of Cranbrook Academy of Art, I visited Saarinen House early in the spring of 1977. Completed in 1930, the house had been used as the home of the president of the academy, and over the years it had been altered and adapted by the different residents in many ways to meet their personal tastes and needs. My first impression of the house was one of endless corridors, rooms, and doors. By the summer of that year, the decision was made to open up the spaces; the partitions and false walls were removed and the interiors painted white.

Like those of my predecessors, my initial intention was to refurbish the house to accommodate my needs, rather than to restore it. During that first visit to the house, the long room in the rear seemed to be an ideal place for my painting studio. My curiosity was aroused, however, when the false walls were removed and the scale of the room revealed. On first experiencing the grandeur of the space, with its dramatic proportions and barrel-vaulted ceiling, I was impressed. Of particular interest to me was the uncovering of the columns, which retained remnants of the paint that accentuated their delicate detailing and fluting. The room was so intimidating and chapel-like that no painter could use it as a studio.

The room was originally a studio, according to Mary Riordan, then curator of Cranbrook Academy of Art Museum, who volunteered to collect vintage photographs of the Saarinen interior. So impressive were the period views of this interior with its carpets, wall hanging, leaded windows, and furniture that I innocently asked, "Why not restore this room?" Mary was almost overcome, for although she had always cherished the idea, no one had ever proposed restoring this work of Eliel Saarinen. So began an undertaking which was to turn eventually into a quest, a search for knowledge on Eliel and Loja Saarinen and Saarinen House. In this venture John Gerard, Mary's colleague and later a curator of the museum, was also most instrumental. The son of teachers at Cranbrook School for boys, John had great sensitivity toward and understanding of Cranbrook. In fact, both Mary and John brought attention to the remarkable architectural drawings and plans by Eliel Saarinen that had been left in limbo, stored in a basement vault, and which proved invaluable in the restoration of the house.

In those early months, Cranbrook seemed to me an architectural oddity, so English in appearance, yet just over twenty miles north of Detroit. How ironic that I, having been born and educated in Wales, would after only a decade in America come to view Cranbrook as an English "home away from home." As far as my knowledge of Saarinen was concerned, I knew only the work of Eliel and Loja's son Eero Saarinen, who had designed Dulles Airport outside Washington, D.C. Having spent ten years at the Corcoran Gallery and School of Art, eventually as its director and dean, I was familiar with the airport's futuristic and sculptural architecture. Without realizing it, moving into Saarinen House signaled for me the beginning of an intense appreciation of the work of Eliel Saarinen.

Dining Room before
restoration, view from
Courtyard. ca. 1983

preceding pages:

Living Room and Dining
Room before restoration.
ca. 1983

My intention was not to come to Cranbrook to restore Saarinen House nor to celebrate Eliel Saarinen, yet both were inevitable. The sheer beauty of Saarinen's architecture became increasingly evident day by day. The orchestration of spaces became a daily enrichment and enjoyment. Eliel Saarinen was a master architect who created breathtaking vistas, manipulating space with unanticipated angles. Likewise, he used decorative elements, whether in brick, stone, metal, or wood, to their full advantage, weaving them into his architecture to enrich and ennoble his final forms. Like all of Cranbrook, Saarinen House was such a visual delight just in its proportions that even with the furniture and furnishings stripped away, the house itself had a certain authority of scale and space.

In the beginning of my residency in Saarinen House, the studio was partially restored, though as the home of the president it was treated as a residence, with a combination of old and new Cranbrook furnishings and sculpture. The original Saarinen dining room furniture was brought out of storage, along with other objects designed by Eliel and Eero for the home. Textiles designed by Loja were placed in the studio. The fireplace in the living room was cleaned and the stunning peacock andirons returned to their rightful place, thanks to the skillful eye of the late Richard Thomas, then head of the Metalsmithing Department. Other furniture designed by former Cranbrook students and faculty, including Florence Knoll, Charles and Ray Eames, and Harry Bertoia, was added, along with additional textiles designed by graduate Jack Lenor Larsen. In this way, Saarinen House became testimony to "Cranbrook Past and Present," a theme that I introduced with the restoration and continued to celebrate during my tenure at Cranbrook, paying tribute to the Saarinen family and to distinguished academy alumni.

Appreciation is due to the individuals who offered expertise and encouragement in the initial partial restoration: designers, alumni, faculty, staff, governors, patrons, and friends. Based on the changes made in Saarinen House, Paul Goldberger, then architectural critic for *The New York Times*, wrote an article titled "Bringing Back Saarinen," which appeared in the spring of 1978 and drew national attention to the restoration, to Eliel Saarinen, and to Cranbrook. The article was a catalyst for curatorial discussions with the Detroit Institute of Arts and the Metropolitan Museum of Art in New York, which culminated in the 1983 international exhibition and publication *Design in America: The Cranbrook Vision, 1925–1950.* The exhibition and book reintro-

"Homage"

Painted by Roy Slade, 1981

Acrylic on canvas, original frame; canvas, 16 x 15 $^{15}/_{16}$ in.; frame, 17 $^{3}/_{8}$ x 17 $^{1}/_{4}$ in.

Gift of Roy Slade, 1994.1

duced Cranbrook and the importance of Saarinen to the world as well as to those who walk its wooded grounds every day.

The house and exhibition gave impetus to restoration projects throughout Cranbrook. Thanks to the efforts of alumni and patrons, the courtyard of the boys' school and the dining room of the girls' school were restored, and much more followed. From interiors to exteriors, the sculpture, and grounds, ongoing restoration has become a responsibility and an opportunity for the entire Cranbrook Educational Community—which today includes not only Cranbrook Academy of Art and Cranbrook Academy of Art Museum but also Cranbrook Schools and Cranbrook Institute of Science—to preserve this architectural masterwork as part of the cultural legacy of our nation.

For me the architecture of Eliel Saarinen also offered personal artistic inspiration. His geometric leaded window designs for the home became the basis of a series of drawings, paintings, and prints I made. The magnitude and magnificence of his talent could be overwhelming, but homage had to be made to Saarinen by one living as a guest in his masterwork. To work on a simple window decoration in its endless variations seemed to be one way to express tribute to his genius.

After years of living in the house, I realized that Saarinen House should be totally restored. The opportunity to make this intention a reality presented itself in 1990, when the head of the Sculpture Department resigned and moved out of Milles House, the adjacent row house named after the Swedish sculptor Carl Milles, who was in residence from 1931 to 1951. Traditionally, the president lived at Saarinen House, while the head of sculpture lived at Milles House. Unlike Saarinen House, Milles House had no furnishings designed by Eliel Saarinen. Though Loja Saarinen had designed textiles for the home, most of these do not survive, and it was decided that the restoration of Milles House would be neither appropriate nor possible. Milles's personal collection of sculptural antiquities that once filled the home are now at Millesgården, his home and studio outside Stockholm, as are the Swedish furnishings that were in the dining room. The spacious interiors could be adapted as the new home of the president, allowing for both individual needs and entertaining, thus permitting Saarinen House to become a museum. In 1992, upon my recommendation, the Board of Governors agreed to the formal accessioning of Saarinen House as an object within The Cranbrook Collection, the core of the permanent collection of Cranbrook Academy of Art Museum. In this way, the house will be subject to the same strict governance and care that is given to the other objects in the collection.

The task of bringing back Saarinen House to its original appearance was eagerly and expertly directed by Gregory Wittkopp, then Curator of Collections, whose quest for excellence is articulated in this book.

Greg's writings display his passion for the house and for perfection in its restoration. The photographs of Balthazar Korab reveal the restored house as a rare treasure, one of the great architectural interiors of our nation.

The true genius of Saarinen was to articulate architecture, art, and nature. To walk through the grounds and buildings at Cranbrook is an endless surprise in the opening up of vistas and views that reveal its unity and coherence. The culmination of his talent lies in Saarinen House itself, with its proportions, strong sense of color, and the array of designed and collected elements that are masterfully orchestrated into a unified whole—in essence, a total work of art. In his philosophy of design, Eliel Saarinen believed that the architect designed everything, from the spoon to the cup to the table to the chair to the room to the house to the street to the city. Saarinen House was a collaborative endeavor of the whole Saarinen family—husband, wife, daughter, and son. Loja supervised all the weaving of the textiles for the home at Studio Loja Saarinen and helped design the gardens. The Saarinens' daughter, Pipsan, created decorative painting designs for the doors in the second floor hallway. Son Eero designed the master bedroom suite of furniture and other pieces throughout the house. The fact that this family of artists could work together so effectively in Saarinen House has enriched the interiors immeasurably.

The most exciting aspect of the restoration to me was the revelation of Eliel Saarinen as colorist. Saarinen trained as a painter, and in early drawings and watercolors his sensitivity to color is obvious. Saarinen clearly enjoyed painting and worked not only in watercolors but also in oil, as is evident from his remarkable portrait of Loja, which hangs in the living room at Saarinen House (see plate 26). Although Saarinen chose architecture over painting, his house is a palette of many hues. Striking are the dramatic contrasts between the rich paneling of the dining room, with its gold dome and bright red niches, the grays and browns of the living room, and the cool greens of the long studio. Throughout the house the thoughtful use of color is evident. To open a closet in the second floor hallway is to reveal a rich turquoise, an unexpected visual delight. But Eliel also incorporated the color of the changing Michigan light, quite similar in intensity to the light of his native Finland, as it spilled into the home through the leaded windows, some of which are tinted with color. The leaded decoration of the windows provides endless delight, like musical variations on a theme. Saarinen also used artificial light to dramatic advantage. The designs of the light fixtures recall the earlier chandeliers and torchères of his Finnish home, yet electric light was used, not candles. The result is that at night Saarinen House takes on a different character, the interior spaces enhanced with washes of warm light, particularly the golden light reflected down into the dining room. The restored Saarinen House can be visually admired as an ever-changing canvas.

As part of the restoration, the Saarinen House garden has been replanted, thanks to the research and guidance of landscape architect and historian Diana Balmori. She has demonstrated the connections between interior and exterior and their relationship to the Arts and Crafts movement. The totality of the experience at Saarinen House and throughout Cranbrook is one of linking the built environment with the natural landscape, an approach that speaks of Eliel and Loja Saarinen's love of nature.

Eliel Saarinen wrote: "It is fundamental that whatever forms a man brings forth...will not be altogether convincing unless they are a true expression of his life—his emotions, his thoughts, and his aspirations. His art, at best, is a significant testimony of his integrity of mind and spirit, the product of his real personality. No work of art in any field can be considered a work of art unless it reveals the basic nature of the artist himself."[1] Saarinen House reveals Saarinen's mind, his spirit, and his aspirations.

The restoration was made possible by the diligent and committed efforts of many individuals, artists, and craftspeople. Particular mention must be made of the encouragement, generosity, and gifts of the grandsons of Eliel and Loja Saarinen, Robert Saarinen Swanson and Ronald Saarinen Swanson. It is my hope that the restored house retains the spirit of the family, not only through their designs and works, but also through the personal objects, books, and art that their descendants have kindly donated and loaned.

Tribute should also be paid to former curator Susan Waller, who, along with Mary Riordan and John Gerard, was instrumental in the restoration of the house and in the growth of The Cranbrook Collection. Named and defined in 1978, the permanent collection is devoted to the work of those artists, architects, and designers who studied, taught, or worked at the academy. The collection helps document the extraordinary influence of these artists throughout the world.

The generosity and vision of Cranbrook's founders, George and Ellen Booth, must also be acknowledged. With their love of the arts and crafts, their unselfish patronage and high expectations, Cranbrook became a reality. George Booth was a visionary who wrote: "We may attain to great reputation in finance and commerce but the enduring proofs of achievement are the standards of beauty we set up for ourselves in thought, word, and deed and the tangible evidences of our devotion to these ideals by the creation of surroundings consistent with such ideals."[2]

Many individuals, particularly his students, have wonderful memories of Eliel and Loja hosting tea parties and mixing martinis, for the house was their home, a place to entertain, talk, and rest. The martinis mixed by Eliel and Loja are legendary, as are the discussions on art, architecture, and design that took place in the studio alcove. Eliel Saarinen was a remarkable man, and his firm opinions and quiet wit influenced many for the rest of their lives. His creative and personal legacies continue to have a profound and lasting impact on those fortunate enough to live and work at Cranbrook. The academy, with almost one hundred fifty graduate students from throughout the world, remains a community of artists: innovative and influential. Today, the grounds and the architecture of the Cranbrook Educational Community by Eliel Saarinen are regarded by critics as "the most enchanted and enchanting setting in America" and "a masterwork of American architecture." In recent years, the praise that has come to Cranbrook is an acknowledgment of the extraordinary genius and vision of architect and founders.

To live in Saarinen House for almost fourteen years was a rare joy, which revealed Eliel's ability to subtly manipulate space, details, and color. Experiencing the harmonious spaces and proportions on a daily basis and witnessing the range of light in the house, which transformed the interiors from dawn to twilight, were ongoing pleasures, ever-changing with the seasons of the year. The dappled greens of spring and summer, the white snows of winter, the golden glow of fall, affected the coloration and mood of the interiors. To open this masterful house, a total work of art, to the public as part of the architectural legacy of our nation has been an honor. Saarinen House will remain as testimony to the architect and his family: the home of genius.

SAARINEN HOUSE: AN ARCHITECTURAL HISTORY

Gregory Wittkopp

INTRODUCTION

To the Finnish-American architect Eliel Saarinen, life and art were inextricably bound within an architectural framework that encompassed all aspects of design. Toward the end of his career he wrote: "architecture embraces the whole form-world of man's physical accommodations, from the intimacy of his room to the comprehensive labyrinth of the large metropolis."[1] While Saarinen was by no means alone in this belief, he had the rare opportunity to develop this ideal, which was at the heart of the Arts and Crafts movement, and the vision to integrate it with the often incongruous goals of twentieth-century modernism. As a designer whose continuing search for form extended from silverware and furniture to buildings and city plans, Saarinen helped pioneer the Arts and Crafts movement in Finland and was a leading proponent of Art Deco and later modernist currents in America.

Saarinen's most thoroughly conceived and harmonious work of art in the United States is Saarinen House, the home and studio that he designed for himself and his family at Cranbrook Academy of Art, where he was both resident architect from 1925 to 1950 and academy president from 1932 until 1946. While Eliel was responsible for the architectural form and most of the furniture, Loja Saarinen, his wife, who headed the academy's Department of Weaving from 1929 to 1942, was responsible for the design of most of the textiles and played an important role in the design of the garden. This collaboration, which was complemented by additional family members as well as other artists and artisans at the academy, resulted in a rare integration of art, architecture, and design: a total work of art.

When Saarinen House was completed, in 1930, it was recognized as a distinct and important contribution to the development of modern American design.[2] In spite of this, the home did not survive

intact after Eliel's death in 1950. It was designated as the residence of subsequent academy presidents, who made numerous changes to the interiors and garden reflecting their changing needs and current styles. By the mid-1970s the house retained only a few hints of its former glory. The large studio had been subdivided into a labyrinth of smaller spaces, the original finishes in the house were stripped or painted over, and the furniture and textiles—so integral to the interiors—were scattered through buildings across the campus.

The restoration began unexpectedly in 1977 with the arrival of Roy Slade, the fifth president of the academy. Like his predecessors, Slade planned to redecorate the house and began by removing false partitions in the studio. Upon seeing the majestic proportions of this barrel-vaulted room and other newly revealed details, he decided that the studio—indeed, the entire house—had to be restored to its original splendor. Under Slade's direction the house was refurbished between 1977 and 1987.[3] The detailed restoration, however, did not begin until 1988 and was concluded in May of 1994, when the house and garden were opened to the public as a historic house-museum operated under the aegis of Cranbrook Academy of Art Museum. The goal of this restoration was to re-create the house and garden—complete in every detail—that Eliel and Loja Saarinen crafted between 1928 and 1930.[4]

To complete the restoration of the interiors a variety of archival sources were consulted, including architectural drawings,[5] historic photographs,[6] period newspaper and journal articles, records of the Cranbrook Architectural Office,[7] as well as the George Gough Booth Papers[8] and the Saarinen Family Papers[9] now in the collection of the Cranbrook Archives. Of particular interest are two inventories that Loja made of the contents of the house: one submitted to the Cranbrook Foundation in 1941[10] and another made shortly after Eliel's death in 1950.[11] In many cases these inventories are the only documentation of objects in the house that do not appear in the historic photographs. Finally, physical evidence found in the house itself during the restoration proved to be extremely valuable, including more than one hundred sixty small paint and wood samples, which were analyzed by Frank Welsh, a historic-paint-color consultant in Bryn Mawr, Pennsylvania.[12]

The decades between the residency of the Saarinens and of Roy Slade were a time when the achievements of Eliel Saarinen were eclipsed by the austere buildings of the International Style. In an era that glorified the glass box, there was little interest in an architecture that drew upon numerous historical precedents to create spaces rich in texture and detail. It was not until 1978, when Paul Goldberger wrote in *The New York Times Magazine* about the start of Slade's restoration, that architects, designers, historians, and critics began to reexamine and appreciate Saarinen House and the American work of this Finnish-born artist.[13] To understand the significance of Saarinen House, however, one must start by examining it within the context of American architecture during the 1920s, a decade when the work of Eliel Saarinen would play an important role moderating the views of modernists and traditionalists.

AMERICAN ARCHITECTURE DURING THE 1920s

By the end of the 1920s American architects, both modernists and traditionalists, believed that their profession was facing a crisis. As Richard Guy Wilson has observed, this crisis came to a boil in 1930 at a symposium on contemporary architecture sponsored by the American Institute of Architects.[14] Modernists like George Howe, who with his partner, William Lescaze, was working on the Philadelphia Saving Fund Society Bank and Office, saw traditionalists as drawing from a grab bag of styles and variously decorating their buildings with the trappings of classical Greek, Gothic, imperial Roman, Italian, French, Spanish, Aztec, Georgian, and colonial motifs. Howe proposed the elimination of eclecticism and encouraged the development of a functional architecture based on the technological advances of science and industry.[15] On the other

side of the debate, C. Howard Walker, a professor of fine arts and an architectural writer, spoke for traditionalists and defended the enduring beauty of ornamentation and the achievements of past cultures.[16]

In between these two factions stood the remainder of the architects who presented papers at the symposium. While all considered themselves modernists and uniformly decried architectural designs that slavishly copied historical styles, they equally opposed the spare forms of European architects like Walter Gropius and Le Corbusier. Ralph Walker, one member of the group, criticized the Europeans' buildings as the work of engineers, not architects. This moderate view of modernism was summarized at the symposium by Harry Cunningham when he commented on the achievements of Bertram Goodhue, one of the most influential American architects at the time of his death in 1924:

> I believe strongly in the effort to develop a reasonable contemporary architecture. I do not, however, agree in any measure with the effort to be radically "modern."

> Nobody ever knew more about tradition than Goodhue did, and nobody was ever more consistently contemporary than he was. You cannot find anything in his [Nebraska State] Capitol, for instance, that is copied, but you can find in his building an echo of every good period the world ever knew. He was contemporary, but he built up his contemporary qualities on all the traditions of all times.[17]

At the 1930 symposium—two years before Henry-Russell Hitchcock and Philip Johnson defined and codified modern architecture as "The International Style"[18]—Cunningham, Ralph Walker, and others spoke for an alternative modernism, one that would form a bridge between the traditionalists and the avant-garde, an architecture that was not intended to be universal in its application but rather a vehicle of specific cultural expressions. It was during this same year and within this context that Eliel Saarinen completed his own home and studio at Cranbrook Academy of Art and opened it to his peers through an article in the December issue of *The Architectural Record,* an issue whose cover featured, significantly, the silhouette of a classical Greek temple superimposed on the steel structural frame of a contemporary skyscraper.[19]

SAARINEN'S DESIGN FOR THE CHICAGO TRIBUNE TOWER, 1922

The debate between modernists and traditionalists and the moderating role played by the work of Eliel Saarinen began in the early 1920s with *The Chicago Tribune*'s celebrated competition to design "the most beautiful and distinctive office building in the world."[20] Announced to architects throughout the world in June 1922, the competition offered $100,000 in prize money and attracted over two hundred sixty entries from twenty-three countries, including Saarinen's entry from Finland (fig. 1). While the majority of the American entries, including the winning neo-Gothic design of John Mead Howells and Raymond Hood, were overtly historical in their conception, many of the European entries, exemplified by the design of Walter Gropius and Adolf Meyer, represented the ideas of the European avant-garde.

These opposing approaches to the design of skyscrapers became a topic of heated debate in the profession. In a 1923 issue devoted to this new architectural form, *The Journal of the American Institute of Architects* presented the debate from the perspectives of an American and a German architect. George C. Nimmons expressed the common American view when he argued that true architecture cannot be expressed through structure but instead occurs through architectural adornment: "If the structure of a skyscraper was honestly and con-

Figure 1

Chicago Tribune Administration Building, Competition Entry, by Eliel Saarinen. Pencil drawing dated 1922; original lost

sistently expressed in the exterior design in the manner proposed by some of the advocates of this policy, it would look like a huge bird cage, and there would not be enough surface left on the exterior to display any architecture whatever."[21] The German modernist Walter Behrendt countered that steel cage construction itself was invented by American engineers and noted: "This form voluntarily renounces the empty pompousness of architectural ornamentation borrowed from the styles of the past, depending for expression not on 'beautiful facade' but on impressive grouping and towering of masses, on harmony of proportions, on forceful effects of interesting outlines."[22]

Saarinen's proposal integrated the strengths of both views. While the arched openings at the street level of the tower and the interior elevations of his observation room at the top echo a medieval past, it is not the overt neo-Gothic detailing of Howells and Hood's design but rather an abstracted reference that demonstrates a sympathy with the neo-Romanesque architecture of Henry Hobson Richardson. The most striking aspect of this design was its soaring verticality, achieved through the elimination of cornices and softened by a series of subtle setbacks. It is a form that Saarinen had been exploring since his proposal for the Finnish Parliament House in 1908, eight years before the landmark New York City zoning law of 1916 made setbacks mandatory there and a common aspect of the urban architectural vocabulary.

Although the only architect sitting on the competition jury voted in favor of Saarinen's entry and the jury as a whole was admittedly struck by the "colossal beauty" of Saarinen's design,[23] the jurors ultimately awarded Saarinen the second prize of $20,000. No doubt there was pressure to select an American architect;[24] furthermore, the jury had a vested interest in Howells and Hood, as they were among the ten architectural firms invited by the organizers and paid to enter the competition.[25]

The fact that the owners of *The Chicago Tribune* sided with the traditionalists should have come as no surprise. From June 1922 through January 1923, *The Sunday Tribune* ran a series of pages giving examples of "architectural achievement through the ages."[26] The presentations were an eclectic mix of buildings from the pages of architectural history—medieval cathedrals, Italian Renaissance palaces, oriental tombs and domed mosques—accompanied by the question: "Is this to be the type of architecture embodied in *The Tribune's* new home?"[27]

It was Saarinen's design, however, that was praised by the critics and was to exert a profound influence on American skyscraper design during the building boom of the 1920s. While Thomas Tallmadge provided the highest acclaim, calling it "the best design since Amiens,"[28] Louis Sullivan offered the most influential observations when he insisted that a true critique of the competition would result in Saarinen's receiving the first prize. In his romantic prose, Sullivan wrote: "The Finnish master-edifice is not a lonely cry in the wilderness, it is a voice, resonant and rich, ringing amidst the wealth and joy of

life. In utterance sublime and melodious, it prophesies a time to come, and not so far away, when the wretched and the yearning, the sordid and the fierce, shall escape the bondage and the mania of fixed ideas."[29] Francisco Mujica called Saarinen's design the "first important crystallization of the modern tendency,"[30] an opinion that Claude Bragdon supported and defined when he described Saarinen's "formula" as "simple, rectilinear masses, the verticals rising sheer without dissenting lines, the elimination of cornices, and general absence of ornament except it be *integral,* in contradistinction to *applied.*"[31] This formula was applied to a host of buildings during the following decade, including quite literal copies such as J. R. Miller and T. L. Pflueger's Telephone Building in San Francisco (1925), and more subtle examples like Raymond Hood's own American Radiator Company Building (1924) and John Mead Howells's Panhellenic House (1928), both in New York, and, in Detroit, Albert Kahn's Fisher Building (1927). Hood acknowledged the influence of Saarinen's design when he wrote: "Goodhue, Corbett, Saarinen and the other men who have given an impetus to the study of this problem, and reproductions of whose drawings were scattered over our tables as we worked, gave us a lift over many rough places."[32] Saarinen's impact on the work of Hood was further confirmed in an interesting postscript to the competition, a letter written by Loja Saarinen to the Finnish architect J. S. Siren in 1955. She notes: "The winner of the 1st prize, Raymond Hood, became one of Eliel's best friends and according to Eero, Hood's Rockefeller Center would not have acquired its shape had it not been for the influence of Eliel."[33]

SAARINEN IN FINLAND, 1898-1923

While Saarinen's entry may have seemed a lonely cry *from* the wilderness to some Americans, he was in fact the leading architect in Finland and known throughout Europe for his projects. Gottlieb Eliel Saarinen was born in 1873 in Rantasalmi, Finland, and studied architecture at the Polytechnic Institute and painting at the Imperial Alexander University in

Helsinki. Although he graduated as an architect, he never entirely abandoned his early dream of becoming a painter. He continued to paint lush landscapes and portraits throughout much of his career and imbued his architectural drawings and completed interiors with an original use of color.[34]

Saarinen first received international attention as the architect of the Finnish pavilion for the Paris Exposition of 1900. He designed it while still a student with his classmates (and later, partners) Herman Gesellius and Armas Lindgren during the last two years of the nineteenth century, a period when the relative political autonomy that Finland had experienced as a Russian Grand Duchy was being undermined by imperial authority. Many prominent artists responded to this attack with works which became symbols of national identity and expressions of political protest designed to elicit international support against the czar's policy of Russification. The ultimate goal of these architects, painters, writers, and composers was not only to obtain political independence from Russia, but also to establish cultural independence from Sweden. Drawing upon the theories and designs of the English Arts and Crafts movement as well as the Vienna Secession and Jugendstil architects, Saarinen and his contemporaries used forms and details derived from Finnish medieval castles, stone churches, and vernacular log structures to create an architectural language that has come to be called Finnish National Romanticism. In the Exposition pavilion, the plan and form recalled Finnish medieval churches, while the interior of the central hall was dominated by frescoes by the Finnish painter Akseli Gallen-Kallela illustrating the mythical events portrayed in the *Kalevala,* Finland's national epic. While Finns no doubt recognized the nationalistic sources of the pavilion's design, the building was a synthesis of national and international styles, including that of the American architect Richardson.

A theme that was central to Saarinen's career in both Finland and the United States, if not the guiding principle, is the belief that architecture encompasses all aspects of design. While many European and American architects at the turn of the century sought to create complete works of art, *Gesamtkunstwerke,* few designed projects as elaborate as the villas Saarinen designed in northern Europe in collaboration with his two partners, including their own country villa, Hvitträsk (1901–03), built during the heyday of their partnership. Situated on a wooded ridge above Lake Vitträsk (White Lake), the complex included a home for each of the partners and a joint studio arranged around a central courtyard. The exteriors of the original buildings (see Balmori, fig. 38) were distinguished by their use of granite and timber, materials indigenous to Finland and which had become symbols of national identity during the National Romantic movement. The timber construction, which recalled vernacular farmhouses, continues in the interior of Saarinen's section, for which he designed or selected a rich variety of applied and decorative arts. The living room, for example, includes carved oak furniture, a *ryijy* rug, and metal candle sconces designed by Saarinen, as well as decorative arts supplied by other artists (fig. 2).[35]

The Finnish National Museum (1902–12), the last project designed under the auspices of the Gesellius, Lindgren, and Saarinen partnership, is the culmination of the National Romantic movement in Finland. The architects won this competition with the argument that each of the museum's departments should be separate and given its own architecturally identifiable form, a concept for which National Romanticism's picturesque and typically asymmetrical style was particularly appropriate. Thus the ecclesiastical art was housed in a space that re-cre-

Figure 2
Hvitträsk, Living Room.
Photographed by Loja
Saarinen ca. 1910

ated a medieval church and the weaponry was placed in a fortresslike tower.

Saarinen's most important project in Europe was the Helsinki Railway Station and State Railways Administration Building (1904–19).[36] Saarinen worked on two of the twenty-one entries submitted to the design competition: one with his partners, Gesellius and Lindgren, the other on his own. His independent entry, called "Winged Wheel on a Globe," a design that was similar in form and detail to the Finnish National Museum, won first place. National Romanticism, however, was no longer the potent symbol it had been, and Saarinen's design was criticized for its adherence to this style. With the Russian czar losing power, Finland had turned to Germany for political support. The alliance was reflected in the new artistic sources Finnish architects began drawing upon, in particular the rational style as it was developing in Germany and Austria.

Saarinen responded to the criticism of his National Romantic design and the changing social context by developing alternative designs for the railway station. He visited railroad stations in Germany, England, and Scotland, and presented a revised design to the railway administration. In the final building, he simplified the exterior forms to boldly reflect the interior spaces dominated by a barrel-vaulted central hall and two slightly lower cross-vaulted halls perpendicular to the entrance hall. The halls are constructed of reinforced concrete, used here for the first time in a major public building in Finland, and finished on the exterior with smooth red granite and faceted mansard roofs. The main entrance, dominated by a semicircular window, is flanked by four monumental sculptures, male figures bearing illuminable globes. Saarinen's artistic sources now included the work of German and Austrian architects, such as the commercial buildings of Alfred Messel and Hermann Billing, Joseph Maria Olbrich's Ernst Ludwig House in Darmstadt, and Josef Hoffmann's Stoclet Palace in Brussels.

The building is not only an important example of early modernism, in which architectural form expresses a building's function, but it is also pivotal in Saarinen's career as the first project where the urban context was an important aspect of the design. City planning, for Saarinen the ultimate *Gesamtkunstwerk* and the subject of one his books,[37] remained a central concern throughout his career, although for the most part economics and politics prevented the implementation of these theories and plans.

SAARINEN IN AMERICA, 1923-28

It was Saarinen's design for the Tribune Tower, however, that brought him to the attention of American audiences and eventually led him to relocate in the American Midwest. No doubt the recession in Europe following World War I and the promise of greater opportunities in the United States were the compelling reasons for Saarinen's first trip to America.[38] With his $20,000 prize, Eliel sailed for New York in February 1923 to see the country and meet with colleagues. He was accompanied by another Finnish architect, Gustaf Strengell, who acted as a translator.[39] In April, Eliel's wife, Loja, and their two children, daughter Pipsan, age eighteen, and son Eero, age twelve, joined him in New York. They moved temporarily to Chicago, staying at the Blackstone Hotel, and eventually to Evanston, Illinois. It was there, without a client in mind, that Eliel began to apply his knowledge of city planning to downtown Chicago, completing a monumental plan for the lakefront.

In the meantime, Eliel's design for the Chicago Tribune Tower continued to receive praise from critics near and far, including a review by Emil Lorch, director of the Department of Architecture at the University of Michigan. In an article Lorch wrote in March of 1923 on the design of skyscrapers, he offered a critique of the Tribune competition, which concluded with the following praise of Eliel's design: "His project is remarkably free of applied and unrelated form and it has beauty to an unusual degree. It rises rythmically and harmoniously from the base upward, modulating subtly to the top; all the masses, planes and lines are in unison as in the master work of the exceptional man who appears only at rare intervals.... If the Tribune competition had done nothing more than to produce this design it would have been well worth while."[40]

This review proved to be most fortunate for Eliel, as revealed in a letter Lorch wrote the following month to his acquaintance the Detroit publisher George Booth, the man who would become Eliel's most important and enlightened patron: "I forgot to say to you yesterday that it is my hope to bring Mr. Eliel Saarinen here for a time next year. By that time he will have a reasonable command of English and since he will be in Chicago, will be quite accessible. His Tribune design practically makes him the leading progressive designer of the architectural world, and as such he belongs here! He has been acclaimed by all the architectural writers who think [of him] as the 'find' of the competition."[41]

By November of 1923 Eliel had accepted Lorch's invitation to join the faculty at the University of Michigan as a visiting professor in architectural design, teaching advanced students. The Saarinens moved from Evanston to Ann Arbor, taking up residence first in the Michigan Union and the following year in a rented home. While there has been some confusion about the duration of Eliel's position in Ann Arbor,[42] the correspondence between Lorch and Booth clearly documents that his position continued through the winter of 1925, although he apparently taught just one semester during each of these two academic years.[43] In a letter dated February 16, 1925, Lorch not only documents the continuation of Eliel's appointment but also shows us the status accorded the Finnish architect:

> The second semester is now under way, and along with, Professor Saarinen's course. For the latter Messrs. Saarinen, Wilby, Rousseau and I selected about a dozen students on the basis of demonstrated interest and capacity. These students thus receive an earned recognition and Mr. S. will have as good a group as we can now

> muster. The other instructors in advanced design have the dubious privilege of keeping the less desirable students without the desired pace-makers. We are all, however, anxious to do what we can to make Mr. S.'s course a success, and by the above selective process we hope to avoid some of the difficulties of last year when some of the "unwashed" got in.[44]

It was at this time that George Booth and his wife, Ellen Scripps Booth, were developing Cranbrook, their home and estate about forty-five miles north-east of Ann Arbor and twenty miles north of downtown Detroit, into a harmonious educational center, the forerunner of today's Cranbrook Educational Community.[45] George Gough Booth (1864–1949) was born in Toronto but later moved to Detroit; he worked as a salesman and designer and eventually became the owner of an ornamental iron-works company in Windsor, Ontario. Early in his career Booth apprenticed as an architect and spent two years in the mechanical trades. Ellen Warren Scripps (1863–1948) was the daughter of James E. Scripps, founder of the *Detroit Evening News.* George and Ellen married in 1887 and in the following year Booth became business manager of the *Evening News,* then general manager, and finally, upon his father-in-law's death in 1906, president of the Evening News Association. Booth remained in this position until 1929, when he retired to devote all his time to Cranbrook. Concomitantly, Booth established Booth Newspapers, Inc., the largest chain of newspapers in Michigan. His personal fortune was based largely on this venture.[46]

From the turn of the century on, Booth had been one of the leading proponents in America of the Arts and Crafts movement. He was a founding member of the Detroit Society of Arts and Crafts in 1906, and was instrumental in the formation of the Society's Art School, which survives today as the Center for Creative Studies. Although as early as 1919 Booth discussed the idea of forming on his estate a community where artists could live and work—an embodiment of the ideals of the Arts and Crafts movement—it did not begin to take concrete form until 1924, when Booth asked Eliel to begin designing a then still nebulous "Academy of Art."

Although it is now clear that it was Lorch who first brought Eliel to the attention of Booth, the question of who cemented this relationship remains the subject of debate. Eliel's biography, which was written with his collaboration in 1946, notes that it was Eliel's student in Ann Arbor and his future son-in-law, J. Robert F. Swanson, who introduced him to George Booth.[47] Albert Kahn, the Detroit industrial architect who designed the Booths' home at Cranbrook in 1907, also claimed the credit, as he details in a 1942 letter to Booth:

> As for Mr. Saarinen you are quite in error as to how he became associated with Cranbrook Institute.
>
> Not that it particularly matters but let me refresh your memory.
>
> You will recall asking me to undertake the preparation of sketches for the proposed Memorial bldg. which you hoped to see placed at the foot of Woodward Ave. [in Detroit]. Because of industrial work on our boards I had to refuse, saying however that I could get you a better man namely Saarinen who had been at Ann Arbor but a short time and very unhappy under Lorch. At that time you were unacquainted with Saarinen, but accepting my recommendation you agreed to have me arrange with him. You as well as all of us were delighted with the results and thereafter you wisely engaged Saarinen to undertake studios for Cranbrook. No one was more pleased than I, for I thought him then and still do today, the outstanding figure in contemporary architecture.[48]

Kahn's letter to Booth was occasioned by Booth's omission of Kahn's name in a public lecture in which he listed the architects and artists who had influenced his life.[49] In any event, Kahn's account is not

accurate, for it is clear from the earlier correspondence with Lorch that Booth was more than "acquainted" with Eliel by 1924, the year Eliel worked on the Detroit riverfront development Kahn mentions in his letter.

In all likelihood, the introduction was facilitated by another of Eliel's students and a friend of Swanson, Henry Booth, a son of George and Ellen Booth. The first meeting of Saarinen and George Booth probably took place on December 8, 1923, at the University of Michigan, where the College of Architecture along with the Michigan Chapter of the American Institute of Architects and the Michigan Society of Architects had arranged a reception in honor of the newly arrived architect. The event included an exhibition of Saarinen's work, a dramatic program titled "A Pageant of Arts & Crafts," written and directed by Henry Booth, as well as speeches by Lorch and George Booth.[50] Both Henry Booth and J. Robert F. Swanson were among Eliel's first students at the University of Michigan, with Swanson, who knew Swedish, serving as a translator for Saarinen, and Henry working on a proposed art academy for Cranbrook as part of his thesis.

Henry's art academy was much more than the hypothetical project of most students and was, in fact, the dream of his father. With the encouragement of Henry, and the recommendation of Swanson and Kahn, George Booth quickly asked Saarinen to help him make this dream a reality. The relationship grew quickly and by the summer of 1924 Saarinen was sufficiently encouraged with the prospects at Cranbrook to cancel his plans to return permanently to Finland.[51] By October Booth had drawings in hand, which he reviewed in his first letter to Saarinen:

> I feel sure that as soon as matters are adjusted You [sic] will be able to work out for me the dreams we have been considering. I have your drawings at my office, and also the topographical

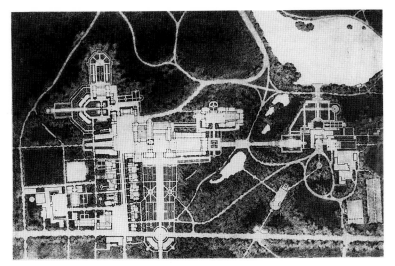

Figure 3
Cranbrook Academy of Art
with Cranbrook House
(right) and Cranbrook School
for boys (left), Proposed Plan,
by Eliel Saarinen. Photostat
of lost drawing dated 1924.
Collection Cranbrook
Academy of Art Museum,
1981.44

*map of Cranbrook, upon which I have made a
slight correction, and I have drawn on this map
for your more ready identification the center
lines upon which your drawing was made. . . .*

*I recall that you stated that you had developed
this plan somewhat at least on the suggestion of
the scheme Harry [Henry] had been working on.
That is, on an axis with the West Terrace of our
gardens. I only wish to say that if you have a
somewhat different vision I hope you will not hes-
itate to feel that the whole territory is open for
you to consider.*[52]

Saarinen did follow Henry's suggestion and used the
axis that runs the length of the West Terrace of the
Booth home, known as Cranbrook House, to define
the northern courtyards of the proposed art academy, a feature that he retained in the final plans as
the Ramp of the Chinese Dog and the walkway
along the north side of the academy museum and
library (fig. 3).

It is important to keep in mind that Saarinen's initial
involvement with Cranbrook was limited, at least in
theory, to the development of plans for an academy
of art. Rather than Saarinen, it was Henry Booth and
J. Robert F. Swanson who developed George
Booth's own sketches and programs of what would
become the first completed buildings of the educational community.[53] After Henry graduated in the
spring of 1924,[54] they established an architectural
practice (called Swanson and Booth) on Cranbrook
Road on the site that later became Brookside
School. Their first projects included several residences in a subdivision just south of Cranbrook as
well as Cranbrook's initial library and architectural
office (1925–26), located on Lone Pine Road. By
the fall of 1924, they had begun to design
Cranbrook School for boys. While it is clear that

Swanson and Booth were
responsible for the development of these initial
Cranbrook projects, both
men admit that Saarinen
nevertheless played a guiding role. Henry recalls that
"Saarinen made sketch plans" for the library and
architectural office, while he and Swanson "made
the drawings for the building." Swanson recalls that
as early as December of 1924, Saarinen was
involved with the boys' school project making preliminary plans based on existing farm buildings.[55]

Although Henry Booth and Swanson encouraged
George Booth to formalize Saarinen's involvement
with these other projects and hire him as the archi-
tect in charge of all building at Cranbrook, George
Booth was hesitant to make a final commitment.
Booth did not want to proceed with any projects
until he was absolutely certain that he had the finan-
cial resources to complete them. The Saarinens
spent the summers of 1925 and 1926 in Europe and
Finland; they returned each September to
Cranbrook, where Eliel worked as a consultant with
Swanson and Booth. However, this situation
changed during the fall of 1926, when Saarinen and
George Booth began to work more directly with
each other.[56]

In an effort to keep the educational projects at
Cranbrook separate from the private projects of
Swanson and Booth, Cranbrook Architectural
Office was officially opened in June 1926 as an inde-
pendent architectural office in the building that
Swanson and Booth had designed. Henry Booth was
in charge of the office and Saarinen no later than
November 1927 was named chief architectural offi-
cer in charge of most new building projects for
Cranbrook. His salary was $1,000 per month, half of
it paid by the architectural office and the other half
coming directly from the Cranbrook Foundation.[57]
From 1926 until the early 1930s, the staff of the
office consisted of almost two dozen people, including architects, designers, tracers, and renderers.
Some were students fresh from the University of

Michigan, and others were veterans of the building trades. The office was responsible for the supervision, inspection, approval, and acceptance of all construction work at Cranbrook, including Saarinen's designs for Cranbrook School for boys (1927–29), the Arts and Crafts Buildings (1928–29), Saarinen House (1928–30), Kingswood School for girls (1929–31), the Academy of Art (1930–38), Cranbrook Institute of Science (1935–38), and Cranbrook Academy of Art Museum and Library (1938–42).[58]

THE DESIGN OF SAARINEN HOUSE, 1928-30

From the beginning, the art academy was conceived as an institution where the teachers and students would live and work together in the same environment. Eliel and Loja's first long-term residence at Cranbrook was one of the original farm buildings designed by Burrowes and Wells in 1912 on the site that would become Cranbrook School for boys.[59] It is unclear whether they first returned to Ann Arbor in the fall of 1925, but a rent receipt indicates they had moved into one of the farmhouses at Cranbrook by December of that year.[60] By 1927, the same time that Eliel remodeled this house, the construction of the boys' school was in full force and their living situation no doubt had become quite unpleasant. The Saarinens moved in with Pipsan and J. Robert F. Swanson, who had married in 1926.[61] The Swansons' house, Towerknoll, which included a large studio apartment, is located on Lone Pine Road about one mile west of Cranbrook. Eliel and Loja remained in this apartment until they moved into Saarinen House in September of 1930.

As early as 1924, Eliel's plans for Cranbrook Academy of Art included a series of faculty houses along Academy Way, the central spine of the academy.[62] The presumed first master plan for the academy (see fig. 3) included row houses and single faculty houses, each with an attached studio, designed around elaborate courtyards. It was not until September 10, 1928, however, that the Board of Trustees of the Cranbrook Foundation authorized the building of residences for both Saarinen and Geza Maroti, the Hungarian sculptor who preceded the Swedish sculptor Carl Milles at Cranbrook Academy of Art.[63] The first dated drawings for Residences #1 and #2, as they would be called on all subsequent drawings, were completed in November 1928,[64] and by February the Cranbrook Architectural Office had received a proposal from Albert Wermuth of Charles R. Wermuth and Son, Inc., to serve as the general contractor for the duplex.[65] Albert Wermuth and his firm, located in Fort Wayne, Indiana, had previously been hired by George Booth to supervise the construction of Christ Church Cranbrook (1924–28) and subsequently served as the general contractor for the boys' school and eventually all of Saarinen's designs for Cranbrook. It was a relationship that worked well and resulted in Eliel and Eero's commission in 1941 to design Wermuth's own residence in Indiana.

During the winter of 1929, Eliel and the architectural office prepared the scale and full size detail drawings for the two residences, a process which took much longer than the contractor had hoped. In June 1929 the contractor wrote: "We are ready to take bids on the Academy Group Residences #1 and #2 with the exception of not yet receiving the specifications for same."[66] By October contracts had been signed with most of the subcontractors, and Wermuth was ready to submit the final estimate for the cost of the two residences, a staggering $135,016.38.[67] This figure reflected the fact that Saarinen specified institutional rather than residential construction techniques. It did not include the cost of the furniture, also paid for by the Cranbrook Foundation, or the textiles, most of which were paid for by the Saarinens. For comparison, the price quoted in September of 1930 in a contractor's advertisement for a brick and stone four-bedroom house, complete with separate dining, breakfast, and sun rooms and a fully plastered basement, was $6,250.00.[68]

The final cost of the Saarinen and Milles residences is not known and it certainly was much higher than the October figure. In all the projects at Cranbrook, Saarinen, and in many cases George Booth, made numerous revisions and changes. Saarinen's own residence was no exception, as noted in a letter from the contractor:

> Please allow us to call your attention to the fact that we can foresee excessive costs on the Academy Group Residences #1 - #2 on account of the delay of not having available revised plans on same. In making this statement we advise you primarily in the interests of our subcontractors who may be involved alone in this particular job. Nevertheless, the job being prolonged, our own costs are involved to such an extent that our guaranteed costs will be influenced.
>
> This is not to be a criticism, however; it is to call your attention to a condition which has arisen in connection with the job.[69]

Although work was progressing on the house throughout the winter of 1929–30, the last drawings for the house were not completed until July, at which time specifications for painting and decorating the walls and ceilings were prepared. As Eliel and Loja were in Finland at this time, their son-in-law sent out these specifications.[70] This appears to have been Swanson's only involvement with the project, with the exception of his designing a few pieces of furniture in the house. By September most of the work was completed for the house's preview in *The Detroit News* on September 14.[71]

THE INTERIOR

The exterior of Saarinen House (fig. 4), as Residence #1 was officially named in the 1950s,[72] does little to forewarn visitors of the remarkable interior spaces, which have been re-created in detail in the restoration. Built of soft-hued Ohio brick[73] and clay roofing tiles finished to imitate the slate used on the neighboring buildings,[74] the residence is part of a varied but unified street facade that includes the adjoining Milles House (Residence #2) to the north, a single house and four row houses on the opposite side of the street, as well as dormitories and studios (fig. 5). While row houses were rare in suburban Detroit, especially for homes of this scale, it is an approach with a long history in Europe and one that Eliel used throughout his city plans. The massing is simple, but not austere, enlivened by the texture and patterns of the brickwork, leaded glass windows set in steel casement frames, and the ceramic roofing tiles.[75] The grade of the front yard is elevated almost

Figure 4

Saarinen House. Photographed June 1934

three feet above the level of the street and defined along the sidewalk by a limestone-capped brick retaining wall, a feature that offers a degree of separation and privacy to the house.

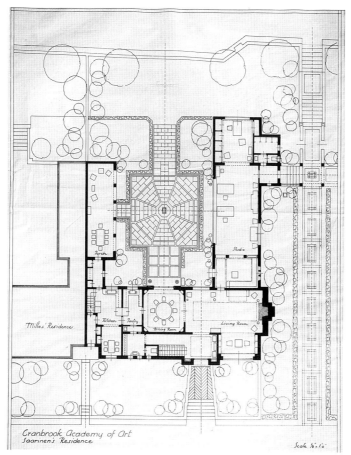

Figure 5
Cranbrook Academy of Art, Academy Way, with Saarinen House (right of automobile). Photographed May 1934

Figure 6
Saarinen House, Proposed Plan of the First Floor. Drawing by Eliel Saarinen, ca. 1928. Ink and pencil on paper; image, 19 ⅝ x 15 ⅛ in. Collection Cranbrook Academy of Art Museum. Gift of Loja Saarinen, 1951.67

distinguished by the handsome oak moldings separating the panes of glass. Guests enter Saarinen House through the front hall, a room that functions both as an entrance foyer and a passage between the social, domestic, and private spaces of the house. Eliel used this space to shield the interior from Academy Way by placing the length of the hall as well as the second floor hallway across the front of the house (fig. 7). This allowed the interior spaces, with the exception of two rooms, to look out to the walled rear courtyard, and thus added to their privacy (fig. 8). The separation of the private realm of the house from the public arena of the street was an important consideration in a community where the students and faculty live and work close to one another. Moreover, the Saarinens in particular had a reputation for being reserved and formal. Eliel subsequently employed this arrangement not only in Milles House and the four faculty residences along Academy Way, but also in the only two single-family residences that he worked on in the United States, the Koebel House in Grosse Pointe Farms, Michigan, which he designed with Eero and J. Robert F. Swanson in 1938, and the Wermuth House in Fort Wayne.

The focal point of the front hall is a large mirror framed with Macassar ebony molding and recessed into the south wall (fig. 9). At some point, presumably after Eliel's death, the mirror was removed and the hole was covered and plastered. It was rediscovered during the restoration when cracks in the shape of a large rectangle were observed in the plaster by project manager Lawrence McLoskey of A Notch Above, the local woodworking firm that implemented the restoration. While the recessed light

The Front Hall

The front door to Saarinen House is approached by a brick walkway, which narrows as it nears the entrance (fig. 6). Eliel used this forced perspective throughout the campus to focus our perception of his architecture. The double front doors, like all the doors at Cranbrook, are unique, in this case

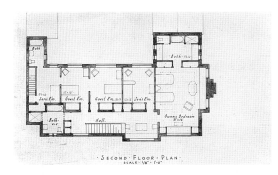

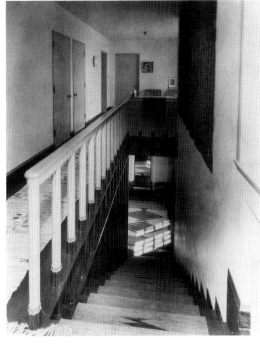

Figure 7
Saarinen House, Proposed
Plan of the Second Floor.
Drawing by Eliel Saarinen,
ca. 1928. Ink and pencil on
paper; image, 7 1/16 x 12 3/16 in.
Collection Cranbrook
Academy of Art Museum,
1980.34

Figure 8
Saarinen House, Courtyard.
Photograph first published in
The Architectural Record,
December 1930

Figure 9
Saarinen House, Front Hall
and Stairway. Photographed
ca. 1930s

fixture above the mirror survived intact under the
later plaster, the mirror itself, plaster details,
and the wooden stop (moldings) and stool (bottom
ledge) were gone. They were re-created from
details noted on a drawing in the Cranbrook
Archives.[76]

The stool of the mirror is low, just eighteen inches
above the floor, and is precisely the same height as a
small table Eliel designed to sit in front of it. The
arrangement is completed by two small benches[77]
on either side of the table and a rug in the center of
the room.[78] Realizing that a visitor's first impression
of the home would be created in the front hall,
Eliel designed an ensemble that summarizes the
aesthetic he employed throughout the entire home.
The tall mirror with the low table is reminiscent of
the Victorian hallstands found in most middle
and upper-middle class homes in America from the
1870s until the 1920s.[79] While Eliel no doubt

rejected their arguably cumbersome form, he nevertheless realized that they served an important
function, allowing a place for residents and visitors
to groom themselves upon entering or before leaving the house. By separating the table from the
mirror and simplifying their design into crisp geometric forms, however, he transformed—rather than
rejected—a nineteenth-century convention, adding
it to his vocabulary of modern design.

The Living Room

Continuing along the axis established by the front
walk and entrance, guests leave the front hall and
pass through a pair of plush velvet portières into the
living room. Like hallstands, portières are a nineteenth-century convention rarely used in the
context of twentieth-century modernism. Yet in the
hands of Eliel and of Loja, the presumed designer of
the fabrics, they become one of the most memorable features of the living room, adding a note of
soft luxury to an otherwise crisp and geometric
space. The Saarinens altered the typical installation
of portières, however, substituting a recessed track

Figure 10
Saarinen House, Living Room
with Book Room (right) and
Studio Alcove (left).
Photograph first published in
The Architectural Record,
December 1930

for the large brass rod and rings common in the previous century. The portières allowed Eliel to design a fairly open first floor plan while maintaining a degree of separation between the spaces, synthesizing old and new traditions.

The initial axis established in the front hall terminates at a globe stand silhouetted in front of a window. Although the window offers a glimpse of the rear courtyard, it is the globe stand that commands our attention.[80] It was designed by J. Robert F. Swanson and executed at Cranbrook in 1932 by the Swedish cabinetmaker Tor Berglund. Fashioned out of rosewood and ebony veneers with stainless steel shelves, its asymmetrical form and cantilevered shelves are reminiscent of the "skyscraper furniture" Paul Frankl designed around 1930, which in turn acknowledged the work of Frank Lloyd Wright.[81] The fact that Eliel selected a globe stand to mark our arrival in the public spaces of his home is significant, symbolizing the Saarinens' view of themselves as global citizens.

It is only after our eyes have come to rest on the globe stand and we turn to our right that we finally have a vista along the main axis of the living room (fig. 10). Eliel established a series of axes throughout the house that permit spaces to unfold in a gradual and often surprising manner. Rather than have us enter the living room along the length of its dominant axis with a focal point, in this case the fireplace, clearly in sight—a principle of Beaux-Arts planning—Eliel leads us along the edge of the room and delays our comprehension of the entire space. Once we turn toward the fireplace, the axis is emphasized by a nineteen-foot rug running the length of the room. The axis is activated, however, by a slight shift in the rug about six inches off the center of the room. The use of shifted and discontinuous axes is a technique

that Eliel used with great skill in his city and campus plans, including both Cranbrook School for boys and Cranbrook Academy of Art, where he even indicated the axes with dashed lines on the preliminary plans.[82] By skewing pathways and causing pedestrians continually to realign themselves to alternate axes, Eliel was able to heighten their awareness of the architectural surroundings. The living room itself is striking in its almost stern simplicity, a space where the careful orchestration of a limited number of elements creates an environment of impeccable harmony. Describing this room, Dr. Wilhelm Valentiner, then director of the Detroit Institute of Arts, observed: "I believe that we have too much clutter in our homes heretofore. We must get used to allowing our eyes to rest on a few unbroken lines and spaces...."[83]

The focal point of the room is the tiled fireplace mantel and a wall hanging on the south wall. The broad fireplace, whose horizontal form is accentuated by its lack of a mantelshelf, was designed by Eliel and executed by the Pewabic Pottery in Detroit under the direction of Mary Chase Perry Stratton.[84] The tiles, which the pottery described as "deep raisin" and "silver" in color,[85] were a dramatic departure for the pottery, which was known at the time for its mottled and iridescent glazes. The tiles were originally executed by the pottery for a dining room Eliel designed for a 1929 exhibition at the Metropolitan Museum of Art, New York. Before the fireplace could be permanently installed in Saarinen House, the width of the facing was shortened by eight inches.[86] At that time the tiles were donated to Cranbrook by Stratton, as a journalist noted, out of an interest in "the modern movement toward the creative design in the field of decorative art in America."[87]

The brown tiles on the face of the fireplace and the dark void of the opening create a dramatic backdrop for a pair of bronze andirons, each consisting of a stylized cock with long tail feathers and a crested head perched on a stepped base. Eliel designed the andirons, like the fireplace, for the exhibition at the Metropolitan.[88] Cocks had been a favored motif of

Eliel during the late 1920s, appearing in his designs for a gate, a rug, furniture veneers, and another pair of andirons. In this instance the cocks clearly represent peacocks, depicted with their tails in profile rather than spread in a fanlike form. Whether or not the Saarinens ever used the andirons is another question. Henry Booth describes Loja as a woman who was so meticulous that she never let Eliel have a fire in the fireplace.[89]

Above the fireplace the Saarinens hung a wall hanging, designed by Loja, depicting a stylized tree. Although trained as a sculptor in Finland, Loja became known in the United States as a designer of textiles.[90] In 1928 she established Studio Loja Saarinen at Cranbrook, a commercial weaving studio, which accepted commissions from George Booth for the buildings at Cranbrook as well as from clients such as Frank Lloyd Wright for Edgar Kaufmann's office in Pittsburgh.[91] The following year George Booth established a separate weaving department at Cranbrook Academy of Art, which Loja eventually headed until she retired in 1942.

The seating in the living room consists of four identical armchairs and a sofa in a formal arrangement that could not have encouraged conversation. Eliel paired two of the chairs on either side of the globe stand, which, with the globe at eye-level, would have prevented people seated in the chairs from seeing each other; the other two chairs were placed at the opposite end of the room, in the corners on either side of the fireplace. The openness of this arrangement is best experienced while standing rather than sitting. Not surprisingly, the original descriptions of this room call it the reception hall or room, not the living room.[92] Eliel seems to have designed the room to receive guests who had been invited to enter the home's public space. With the exception of large gatherings such as the annual teas, when the room was filled with both standing and seated guests, and the seating would be supplemented by metal chairs with wicker seats, Eliel and Loja no doubt preferred meeting with guests in the more intimate spaces, including the book room, dining room, or studio alcove.

The sofa, with its *ryijy*-rug draped bench, is a direct quotation from Hvitträsk (see fig. 2), which in turn was a quotation from Eliel's Finnish Pavilion in Paris. Gallen-Kallela, the Finnish painter responsible for the murals in the pavilion, also designed a *ryijy* rug in 1899 for a display there.[93] Titled "The Flame," the rug was the first modern Finnish adaptation of the centuries-old Scandinavian weaving technique that uses knotted wool pile. The rugs, originally a substitute for animal pelts,[94] became one of the many traditional Finnish crafts revived during the National Romantic movement. Eliel was an important collector of antique Finnish *ryijy* rugs, and they were a primary influence for Loja, who used the same technique to weave the rugs she designed in Finland and at Cranbrook, including the sofa cover and the rug for the living room of Saarinen House.

The only other piece of furniture in the room is a low cabinet or bookcase located between the book room and the doorway to the front hall. The cabinet, as well as the chairs, sofa ends, globe stand, and the furniture in the front hall, were all designed by Eliel and executed at Cranbrook by the Swedish cabinetmaker Tor Berglund (fig. 11).[95] In 1927, when George Booth established the Cranbrook Foundation as the governing body of the educational community, he made provisions for both an Academy of Art and a School of Arts and Crafts. Although the academy did not open until

Figure 11
Cranbrook Arts and Crafts Studios, Cabinet Shop, with Tor Berglund. Photographed ca. 1930

1932, the crafts studios opened in the fall of 1929 with the appointment of a printer, weavers, an ironworker, a bookbinder, a metalsmith, and a cabinetmaker. Saarinen was fortunate to have all of these artisans at his disposal, in particular Berglund, whose veneered cabinetry and case goods are integral to the interiors of the house. Before coming to Cranbrook, Berglund worked with Carl Malmsten, who in 1916 won the furniture competition for the new City Hall in Stockholm.[96] Berglund remained at Cranbrook until August 1932, when he returned to Stockholm,[97] and the cabinetry studio closed. With the opening of the academy and the toll taken by the Depression, the remainder of the crafts studios closed in 1933.

For the living room, the Saarinens initially selected three works of art to hang on the walls: Loja's wall hanging above the fireplace, an oil portrait of Loja by Eliel to hang above the cabinet or bookcase, and a gouache drawing by the Finnish artist Helene Schjerfbeck to hang asymmetrically above the sofa. Saarinen once observed, "To paint a picture is art, to hang it is architecture."[98] While most of the artwork in the house is placed in expected locations, the Schjerfbeck is an exception, not centered above the sofa but placed above the left arm and decisively close to the studio entrance. The placement of this picture defies common rules of interior design, yet, like the rug, which is six inches off center, the framed drawing completes the composition of the east wall, serving as a transition from the low sofa to the tall narrow doorway. Sculpture in the room initially included a ceramic by the Russian artist Mikhail Vrubel (fig. 12) and later a small Aztec-style carving that sat on the thin top edge of the tile fireplace mantel.[99] Of all the sculpture in the house, the *Sea Princess* by Vrubel was given the most prominence in its display, with a veneered pedestal bearing an identification label.[100]

The living room is the darkest space in the house and most reminiscent of the cavelike quality of the central living spaces of Hvitträsk. This effect is achieved through the controlled use of natural light and the selective use of incandescent light, in this case indirect light that reflects off the ceiling from three bronze torchères. Throughout the major spaces of the house, Saarinen preferred to light the rooms with torchères or hanging fixtures that provide a soft, uniform, indirect light, rather than conventional fixtures, which give off a harsher light. The room is further dimmed by the use of jute cloth on the walls, an adaptation of the natural grass-cloth made from sea grass that Saarinen used in Hvitträsk. Wallcovering was important to Saarinen's conception of the room, and during the family's residency he used two different materials. In 1930 he took traditional grass-cloth and modernized it by introducing synthetic materials that could be woven by machine. An article in *House Beautiful* describes the material originally used on the walls as a "fabric of rayon and jute . . . woven especially for this room by the Dupont Company."[101] By September 1936 this fabric had been replaced by a commercial jute-cloth, as glimpsed in a photograph published in *Pencil Points* (see fig. 29) and analyzed from a fragment found during the restoration.[102]

The Book Room

Many of the theories Eliel applied to city planning in general and the art academy master plans in particular, including what he called in another context "intimate, painterly settings within the network of roads and open spaces,"[103] are evident in the plan for Saarinen House. The book room, an alcove to the right of the fireplace with a large window facing the street, becomes the intimate retreat off the open space of the living room (fig. 13). In this space Eliel or Loja had quiet conversations or enjoyed afternoon tea with a guest while sitting in the two large lounge

chairs. It is also the room where Loja often sat during the day to work on the clothes she designed for herself.[104]

Behind the lounge chairs are bookshelves which, like the woodwork in the living room, are maple stained gray.[105] The shelves are lined with the Saarinens' leather-bound books whose browns, golds, and maroons complement the rust and gold yarns in the upholstery Loja designed for the chairs in the book room and living room. Like many educated Finns, the Saarinens were conversant in Finnish, Swedish, German, and English, and their library included volumes in all four languages, many of which were purchased as paperbacks and bound as hardcovers in Helsinki. The backdrop for the book room is a pair of linen curtains hanging in front of the large window that overlooks Academy Way.[106] Like all the curtains Loja designed for the house, these have a translucence that softens without obscuring the view toward the street. Throughout the house Loja used a combination of sheer cotton voiles and handwoven fabrics, which most of the historic photographs show drawn across the windows. Consequently, the translucence of these curtains is a critical component of their design, providing a degree of privacy while maintaining a link between the interior and exterior. On the window ledge, which functions as a radiator enclosure, the Saarinens kept a collection of art objects purchased in the 1930s from Austrian, Hungarian, Finnish, and French artists. The one surviving object by an American artist is a ceramic sculpture titled *Young Pegasus* by Viktor Schreckengost. In the case of at least this object, it was Loja, not Eliel, who purchased the work directly from the artist.[107] A more densely woven band at the bottom of the curtains creates a backdrop for these objects.

The Dining Room

The dining room is not only the most elaborate room in the house but also the space that exemplifies in plan and detail Eliel's belief that architecture encompasses all aspects of design (fig. 14). Ironically, it is also the room that suffered the most changes after Eliel died in 1950 and Loja moved out of the house in 1951. Historic photographs and early magazine and newspaper articles describe an octagonal room with wood paneling, four corner niches painted a brilliant Chinese red, and a golden dome in the ceiling, elements which were no longer visible at the beginning of the restoration.

The most critical and challenging aspect of the restoration of the dining room was the identification and reproduction of the veneered plywood paneling. Although the original blueprints provide thorough documentation of the house, they do not specify surface treatments such as wood finishes and paint colors. Furthermore, Eliel often made changes to his designs as they were being constructed, adjusting proportions and decorative details. Thus the blueprints were a starting point but could not be considered definitive. In the case of the paneling, the plans simply specify the use of "3 ply panels." The article in *House Beautiful* offers a little more information, noting that the walls were covered with "natural fir panels."[108] A series of letters in the Cranbrook Archives finally shed light on this mystery. The first letter was sent on behalf of the general contractor, Charles Wermuth, to the Cranbrook Architectural Office.[109] The general contractor seemed to be having difficulty locating the "small straight-grained fir" that Saarinen specified in the bulletin and asked if a substitution such as rotary-cut fir could be used. On

Figure 13
Saarinen House, Book Room, with Lilian Swann Saarinen, Eero's first wife (left), and Loja Saarinen. Photographed early 1940s

Figure 14
Saarinen House, Dining Room. Photographed after 1935

Figure 15
Saarinen House, Dining
Room Table with Tablecloth,
designed by Loja Saarinen.
Photographed May 1935

the following day, the architectural office sent their
emphatic response: "Dining
Room panelling must be
straight sawn veneer. No
rotary cut veneer will be
accepted, no matter how selected. This material was
used for panelling on the Head Master's Residence,
and no question was ever raised about supplying
it."[110] The original headmaster's residence across the
street shares many details with Saarinen House,
including the use of rift-cut straight-grained fir paneling and a Pewabic fireplace mantel.

One more question about the panels remained to be
answered: How did Eliel finish the fir veneer?
Although the panels that form the grid on the walls
had been removed in the 1960s and replaced with
wallboard, the room's original base and crown moldings and four corner niches remained in place.[111] On
a piece of original molding from one of the niches, a
microchemical test with squaric acid detected calcium in a white film residue on the surface on the
wood.[112] Based on formulas published in manuals
from the period on wood finishing, the presence of
calcium indicated that the wood had been bleached
using a caustic solution of lime and possibly soda.[113]
This treatment was unusual in 1930, but its effect
was later imitated by a much simpler technique pop-
ularly known as pickling.

The culminating architectural feature in the dining
room is the central gilded dome with three sur-
rounding rings.[114] At some point, a subsequent
resident painted over the gilding with white paint. It
was regilded by William Adair in 1990 using the
original techniques and materials, in this case
twenty-three-karat gold leaf. Indirect lighting is
employed with great drama through a brass lamp
suspended below the gilded dome. The circular
shade is divided into eight segments and thus serves
to integrate the geometries of the circular dome
and the octagonal plan of the room. Directly below
the gilded dome and the brass lamp is a circular din-

ing room table which, along with its chairs, is one of
the most celebrated Art Deco designs in America.[115]
Designed by Eliel and made by the Company of
Master Craftsmen, a division of W. and J. Sloane in
New York, the table and fourteen chairs are the only
pieces of wooden furniture in the house not made by
Tor Berglund at Cranbrook. Eliel was disappointed
with the company's decision to paint rather than
inlay veneers, as reflected in the following letter
from W. and J. Sloane to Saarinen:

> In regard to painting the lines on the chairs
> instead of inlaying; this was done in our factory
> after the most careful study by Mr. Rock and
> myself of the most feasible way of giving you the
> effect you desired. It proved to be physically
> impossible to do this with the insertion of the
> inlay in the fine lines shaped in accordance with
> the curve of the chairs. We felt positive that the
> durability of the work and the satisfaction that
> you would obtain would be much greater by car-
> rying it out as we have done rather than by taking
> very great chances in trying to carry out the fine
> lines of the inlay in such narrow widths on curves.
> Therefore, I took the responsibility of having the
> lines painted.[116]

Eliel was a perfectionist and, as indicated in the earlier letter to the general contractor regarding the
rift-cut fir paneling, not willing to accept the easy
solutions, especially when he knew the quality of
work that Berglund was capable of producing at
Cranbrook. Even with their painted black and gold
lines, the chairs are one of the most striking designs
in the house.

In its standard configuration, the circular table had a
diameter of fifty-eight inches and could comfortably
seat six people. However, for larger dinner parties,
Eliel designed four leaves for the table that allowed
it to expand to seventy-one inches and accommodate at least twelve chairs (fig. 15). Whereas most
circular tables are expanded by pulling apart the
two halves and inserting rectangular leaves, the
leaves for this table are quarters of a ring that slide
into the perimeter of the table, maintaining its circu-

lar form. Since the leaves were not veneered, Loja designed a coral-colored linen table cloth, shaped like a doughnut, that covered the leaves but not the veneers on the center of the table.

Eliel was a leading proponent of Art Deco as it developed in the United States. Three years after Eliel and Loja visited the *Exposition Internationale des Arts Décoratifs et Industriels Modernes,* the 1925 show in Paris that inaugurated and named the style,[117] Eliel was asked to design a dining room for the exhibition at the Metropolitan Museum of Art, New York, titled *The Architect and the Industrial Arts: An Exhibition of Contemporary American Design* (fig. 16). This pivotal exhibition gave formal approval to the Art Deco style in the United States. For it, Eliel designed the dining room, served as the design consultant for the entire exhibition, and contributed an essay to the catalogue titled "Modern Features of Art."

In one of the first critical discussions of Art Deco, Rosemarie Haag Bletter contrasts the style with the developing International Style and describes Art Deco as a popularized modern style, one that is not "an overtly revolutionary style or a total break with the past."[118] If, instead of using this definition in a derogatory manner that posits the International Style as the more "advanced style,"[119] we view Art Deco as creating an alternative modernism, one that builds upon the achievements of the past and synthesizes numerous sources to create new and original designs, it is easy to see how Eliel's work would epitomize the style. Indeed, one of the sources for Art Deco that Bletter cites is the National Romanticism that Eliel helped to define in Finland.[120]

Eliel incorporated several items from the Metropolitan dining room into Saarinen House. He used the Pewabic fireplace tiles and the peacock andirons in the living room, and the rug in the dining room. Like the dining room furniture, the rug was not made at Cranbrook but rather machine-woven in

Philadelphia.[121] Although no correspondence survives with the rug's manufacturer, Barrymore Seamless Wiltons, it was probably woven in the fall of 1928 at the very time Eliel was beginning to design the house.[122] The rug plays an important role in the design of the house. Its octagonal pattern refers to the plan of the room, and Eliel repeated a similar pattern in his design for the courtyard outside the dining room. Likewise, the overall dimensions of the

Figure 16
Dining Room by Eliel Saarinen for *The Architect and the Industrial Arts* at The Metropolitan Museum of Art, New York, 1929

dining room, which one can argue were determined by the dimensions of the rug, become a module in the plan of the house. The living room, for example, is the same width and approximately twice the length of the dining room.

On the west wall of the dining room is a tapestry designed and woven by the Finnish artist Greta Skogster. Measuring almost seven feet high by ten and one half feet wide, the tapestry depicts elements from a landscape, including a tree and four birds, all of which are about life-size. The effect in the room is that of a mirror, one that symbolically reflects the landscape outside the doors on the

Figure 17
Saarinen House, Dining
Room, with Loja Saarinen.
Photographed ca. 1942

Figure 18
Saarinen House, Dining
Room. Photograph first pub-
lished in *The Architectural
Record*, December 1930

opposite wall. As Diana Balmori discusses in her essay, the tapestry is an important element in an axis that begins in the dining room and ends in the woods on the other side of the Triton Pool. However, we must also take into account the axis that is perpendicular to this one and leads from the dining room through the living room to the fireplace. At the junction of these two axes is the dining room table on which Eliel positioned, at the very center, a silver bird (fig. 17). Although Eliel did not design this object, he or Loja carefully selected it for the space, and Eliel may have had the base of the bird altered to match the circular pattern at the center of the table, as the size of these two circles is too similar to be coincidental.

The bird is also a cock of some type, although clearly not a peacock like those Eliel incorporated into the living room andirons. Alexander Tzonis suggests that the bird represents the metso, a large wood-grouse or blackcock found in Finland.[123] Tzonis, in his discussion of Reima Pietilä, the contemporary Finnish architect who used the metso as an inspiration for the plan of the Tampere Main Library, notes that according to Pietilä, "the wood-grouse, which lives in the 'deep primeval woodlands' of Finland, has become 'the *genius loci*' for the Finnish people.'"[124] Even if this silver bird, which was designed by an Austrian artist, does not actually represent a metso, it is tempting to believe that for the Saarinens it symbolized one, positioned as it is on the fulcrum of the axes that represent the interior and the exterior, home and nature.

One of the most poetic descriptions of the dining room as it appeared to the Saarinens' contemporaries, and one of the best testaments to its conception as a total work of art, was written by a journalist visiting the house in 1942:

> The dining room is at the left of the entrance and gleams a golden welcome to guests. Light is reflected from a gilded dome ceiling back to the top of the round table made of rays of harewood inlaid with ebony in a way that suggests the sun. Places are set on circular doilies of yellow linen blocked with black figures which the Saarinens' son, Eero, made when he was a child. On these are black plates, on these folded yellow napkins and on top of these yellow cups and saucers. Each guest unpiles his cup to get his napkin as the plump brass coffee pot is brought around. It's delicious coffee and amber enough as it streams from the slender spout to fit into the color scheme.
>
> Mr. Saarinen looks vastly amused when he tells us the chairs, with their Spanish comb look and sunny as the table itself, are made of hollywood. He has designed them as he has the other furniture in the house, and they are dramatic. The walls of this golden room, seeming sunny on a gray and snowy day, are of waxed California pine. One of them is nearly covered with a Finnish tapestry made by Greta Skogster in soft terra cotta tones. The ombre [sic] shaded carpet is creamy white and brown.
>
> A pineapple upside down cake is part of the edible harmony, but Mrs. Saarinen refuses to admit she serves food to carry out the architectural scheme.[125]

While the cake may not have been an official part of the architectural scheme, everything else in the room complemented its golden glow. The coral-colored horsehair upholstery as well as the rust and gold woven side panels, used on both the windows overlooking the courtyard as well as the dining room side of the portières, are believed to have been designed by Loja and woven in Studio Loja Saarinen (figs. 18, 19).[126] Their weave allows them to be translucent during the day and reflective at night, adding to the golden glow of the room. In the niches were metal objects designed by Eliel, such as the coffeepot from Hvitträsk described by the journalist; objects selected by Eliel, such as the creamer and sugar bowl designed by Jan Eisenlöffel;[127] and antiques the Saarinens brought with them from Finland. On the wall to the left of the entrance to the pantry hung a Japanese wood-block print.[128] As late as May of 1930 Eliel had intended to enclose the four niches with glass doors framed in polished bronze.[129] Although the four frames were executed, two of which survive in storage at the art museum, they never were used. Their weight alone would have made installation extremely complicated since they require more support than the final design of the niches permits.

In the center of the north wall of the dining room is a swinging door leading into the pantry. The pantry, which contains a refrigerator (powered by a motor located in the basement), dish sink, glass-faced cupboards, Monel-faced counters, and a slop sink, also had a door that connected it to the coat room and the front hallway.[130] Beyond the pantry is the kitchen, from which hallways lead to both the basement and the rear porch of the courtyard (fig. 20), and a stairway leads upstairs to the maid's bedroom. As little documentation and no photographs exist for the kitchen, this room and the connecting hallways have not been restored. Our only knowledge of their content is from Loja's 1950 inventory, where she notes that one black Formica table and two folding chairs

belonged to Cranbrook and would remain in the kitchen, as well as four easy chairs, four small tubular chairs, two small tubular tables, and one large table with a black Formica top, which would remain on the rear porch (fig. 21).[131] The floors in the pantry and kitchen were covered with carmel-colored battleship linoleum.

The Saarinens always had a housekeeper, typically a young woman from Sweden. The second housekeeper was Anna Danielson, who worked in Saarinen House from about 1931 to 1937.[132] As a single woman, she lived in the house, occupying the maid's bedroom at the top of the kitchen stairway. After she married, in 1933, she continued working at the house during the day and left after she had prepared dinner. She recalls that most of the subsequent housekeepers did not live in the house. Danielson's responsibilities included preparing all meals, both cooking and baking, and light cleaning. Although the Saarinen's chauffeur and handyman was responsible for the heavy cleaning, such as the kitchen floors, she was the only person who cleaned the upstairs. Most of the laundry was sent out, and she was responsible for washing just the "delicates."

On a typical day, Danielson prepared breakfast and carried it to a table in the

Figure 19
Saarinen House, Dining Room, during a party for students. May 11, 1946

Figure 20
Saarinen House, Porch and Courtyard. Photograph first published in *The Architectural Record*, December 1930

Figure 21
Saarinen House, Porch, with Loja Saarinen (center left), Robert Swanson (center right), and Eliel Saarinen. Photographed ca. 1943–44

Figure 22
Saarinen House, Studio
Alcove. Photograph first
published in *The Architectural
Record,* December 1930

Figure 23
Saarinen House, Studio
Alcove, during a party for
students. May 11, 1946

Figure 24
Hvitträsk, Dining Room.
Photographed after 1914

second floor hall-way at precisely 7:30 A.M. Lunch would be served exactly at noon in the dining room. As breakfast was light, lunch would be quite substantial, but the main meal was dinner, which was served at about 6:00 in the dining room. At 4:00 every day, afternoon tea would be served, although the Saarinens always drank coffee. The location varied, but Danielson often served it in the book room unless there was more than one guest, when it would be served in the dining room. In warm weather, tea as well as the other meals would be served on the rear porch of the courtyard, which until the late 1970s still had its original screens. George Booth or a colleague from the art academy would often be the guest for tea.

The Studio Alcove

The transition between the living room and the studio is the studio alcove (fig. 22). Eliel defined this alcove, although part of the spacious studio, as a separate space by lowering the height of the ceiling and screening the alcove from the remainder of the room with a colonnade of fluted piers and pilasters. The transitional nature of this space, linking the personal and professional realms of the house, is most evident in the subtle change in the floor level. Whereas the main portion of the studio is one step down from the rest of the first floor, the floor in the alcove continues at the level of the living room. Consequently, this space functions as an alcove off both the personal space of the living room and the professional environment of the studio.

Family members, colleagues, and students alike speak of this alcove as the heart of the house, the place where Professor Saarinen occasionally invited a student to meet with him to discuss his or her most recent project, where Eliel could entertain a client, where Eliel and Loja retired after dinner to continue their conversations, and where their grandchildren played with the dolls that Pipsan and Eero had as children at Hvitträsk (fig. 23).[133] Loja often referred

to this space as the "cosy corner," a name that captures its intimate nature.[134] In 1937 Florence Davies, the art critic at the *The Detroit News,* observed that "the great sunny studio, an integral part of the house, remains as ever the social center of the household, since often after-dinner guests instinctively wander on through the drawing room to the small lounge or conversation center at one end of the big studio, because this room seems to be the most vital place in the house."[135]

The alcove is dominated on two sides by a built-in bench with a back made of oak panels. The seat is draped in a geometrically patterned *ryijy* rug down to the floor level; two separate *ryijy* rugs with similar but distinct patterns cover the dark oak parquet floor. Twelve green velvet-covered cushions line the seat back.[136] Like the sofa in the living room, this *ryijy*-draped bench recalls a similar installation at

Hvitträsk, in the alcove between the living and dining rooms (fig. 24). Whereas the pattern of the *ryijy* that Eliel designed and used in Finland is a narrative description of life in Hvitträsk, depicting, for example, Loja with her flowers, Pipsan crowned as a fair-haired princess, and the young Eero with his beloved animals,[137] the *ryijys* that Loja designed for Saarinen House, including the alcove, are not narrative but rather incorporate geometric patterns that are reminiscent of Eliel's architectural detailing, including the brick courtyards and walkways at Cranbrook. Eliel used a similar pattern in the veneered surface of the occasional table in the alcove.[138]

The intimate, indeed cozy nature of the studio alcove is enhanced by the leaded colored glass Eliel used in the windows and doors, a feature limited in the house to this space. Although Eliel's preference was to use leaded clear glass throughout the buildings at Cranbrook, he occasionally incorporated colored glass. When he did, however, the glass had a soft tint, in this case pale yellows and greens. So subtle is the color that the glass suggests the presence of green foliage outside the window rather than a color in the glass itself. In this respect Eliel blurred the distinction between the interior and exterior, creating a quiet transition.[139] Like the *ryijy* rugs on the floor, the glass incorporates a geometric pattern, here a triangular motif that is a more complex variation on the simple triangles incorporated into the leaded clear glass used throughout the second floor of the house.

The paintings Eliel and Loja initially selected for the wall include an unidentified painting of a female nude and a portrait of Eliel's father, both of which are missing. Gradually these were replaced by paintings by two of the Saarinens' colleagues at the art academy, Zoltan Sepeshy and Wallace Mitchell, as well as Eliel's sketch for the tapestry that Studio Loja Saarinen wove for Eliel's church in Columbus, Indiana (fig. 25). The painting by Sepeshy, titled *Landing in New York,* shows an ocean liner arriving in the New York harbor, a subject that held special meaning to both Sepeshy and the Saarinens as European immigrants to the United States.

The Studio

The studio alcove overlooks the main portion of the studio, a barrel-vaulted space over forty-seven feet long that includes another alcove at the east end, which Eliel used as his office (fig. 26). As the name implies, the studio was the space that Eliel used to work on his architectural projects when he was not working in the Cranbrook Architectural Office across Academy Way or later in the office he and Eero shared on Long Lake Road. Eliel furnished the space with three drafting tables of his own design, presumably so that he could be working on several drawings simultaneously, a credenza with a top that pulled out to display large documents, seven of the tubular metal chairs Eero designed for the auditorium of Kingswood School for girls, an upright piano, and a "bar buffet" designed by J. Robert F. Swanson. Cocktails were an integral aspect of the Saarinens' life in Saarinen House and the cocktail hour an important opportunity to relax. The art museum's director at that time, Albert Christ-Janer, who wrote Eliel's biography, noted: "At five o' clock he would have tired of detailing these personal recollections and professional developments; his slightly slanted, deeply hooded blue eyes would sparkle and he would say with relief, 'Ah, the cocktail hour, the happiest hour of the day. Loja, now we can have martinis!' "[140]

Figure 25
Saarinen House, Studio Alcove, with Svea Kline and Eliel Saarinen during a tea party in front of *Sketch for the "Sermon on the Mount Hanging."* May 18, 1945

Figure 26
Saarinen House, Studio, with *Cartoon for the "Sermon on the Mount Hanging."* April 7, 1941

Figure 27

Saarinen House, Studio and
Studio Alcove.
Photographed ca.
September 1930

Figure 28

Cranbrook Academy of Art,
Studio Loja Saarinen,
weavers (left to right)
Elizabeth Edmark, Marie
Bexell, Mrs. John
Buckberrough, and Gerda
Nyberg, with the "Exhibition
Rug" on the floor.
Photographed May 1935,
first published in *The Detroit
News*, May 12, 1935

Figure 29

Saarinen House, Studio.
Photograph first published in
Pencil Points, September
1936

On the walls Eliel displayed an ever-changing selection of his architectural drawings, primarily presentation renderings of his earlier projects in Finland. On the north wall, for example, nearest the alcove, hung a large elevation detail of the entrance to the Helsinki Railway Station (fig. 27). As Loja returned most of these drawings to Finland after Eliel's death, the current restoration uses Eliel's renderings of his buildings at Cranbrook. Throughout the Saarinens' residency, an antique Finnish *ryijy* rug hung on the south wall, part of Eliel's collection that also included the two that hung in the stairway leading to the second floor (see fig. 9).[141]

Although the studio functioned primarily as a working space, Eliel and Loja also used it to entertain the faculty and students of the academy on occasions such as the annual tea party that they hosted each May at the time of graduation. For these events the three drafting tables were removed to accommodate the guests. In 1933 Studio Loja Saarinen finished weaving a large *ryijy* rug that Loja designed for this space, a rug similar in color and pattern to those in the adjacent alcove (fig. 28). Called the "Exhibition Rug," it appears in just one historic photograph of the studio, although the Saarinens used the rug in the studio for many large formal parties (fig. 29).[142] The rug is the only one in the house that was paid for by the Cranbrook Foundation, although on Loja's invoice she noted that she was reducing the price by thirty percent, as there was "no charge for design and supervision."[143] In spite of the rug's limited use in the house, it evidently was quite important to Loja, and after Eliel's death she negotiated

with Henry Booth, then president of the Cranbrook Foundation, to be able to take the rug and the three others in the studio alcove to her new home. Booth responded to her offer with the following comments:

> I have considered your propositon of trading all the rugs you own with the exception of the cozy corner rug and settee rug for the big "exhibition" rug which has been used in the studio from time to time.
>
> As far as I am able to determine the proposed trade is equitable. If you still feel that it is, we are agreeable to the proposition and shall consider the matter settled unless we hear from you.
>
> The large rug is now on the floor in the "Headmaster's House" where you may see it if you wish.[144]

At the east end of the studio Eliel created a second alcove, his office, by again lowering the ceiling height and narrowing the width of the space (fig. 30). In the exact center of this space Eliel placed his desk, its length on the axis of the length of the studio. With this arrangement, Eliel could sit at his desk with commanding views of the landscape to his left and his architecture to the right. Behind him a recess in the wall was filled with flat files that he used to store photographs of his buildings and his architectural drawings.[145] In front of him was a built-in cabinet for his Philco radio. This cabinet as well as the closet on

its left were only rediscovered when the studio was restored in 1988, for the entire east wall of the office alcove had been covered by a layer of wallboard. The doors from the closet were being used to create a makeshift closet where the recess for the flat files is located. The fact that Eliel designed the smaller cabinet to house a Philco radio was noted by Robert Saarinen Swanson, the Saarinens' grandson, who recalls the radio during his visits as a child.

The oak radio cabinet has a much lighter finish than the oak woodwork throughout the remainder of the studio, and apparently Eliel added it at a later point, perhaps in the early 1940s, when he used this lighter finish on the oak woodwork in the academy's art museum and library.[146] The separate nature of the alcove was reinforced by Loja's curtains, which were accented with yellow rather than green as were those in the central portion of the studio.[147] A solid yellow pile rug was used on the floor under the desk.[148]

Whereas the long window along the north wall is an expected feature in a working studio of this size, the large east and south windows are unusual. Direct sunlight was evidently as important to Eliel as the uniform light obtained from a northern exposure, a fact that so impressed his patron, George Booth, that he felt compelled to convey it in a letter to Emil

Lorch: "Mr. Saarinen regards it as a distinct error that any room in which we work should not have a chance to receive the sunlight at least a portion of the day."[149] Although the living room and the cozy corner are memorable for their dimness, it is also true that every room in the house, including the bathrooms, is designed to receive direct sunlight for at least part of the day.

A door at the southeast corner of the studio leads into a small vestibule. While the green tile on the floor matches the tile used on the window sills in the studio, and the green and gray paint on the walls is similar to the palette used for the textiles in the studio alcove, the groin-vaulted ceiling, painted a bright yellow ocher, is a dramatic touch. Although simplified, the vaulting recalls the plasterwork Eliel employed in his villas in Finland at the turn of the century, including Suur-Merijoki and Hvitträsk. The ocher color is common throughout Finland, where it is used on both the nineteenth-century Neoclassical buildings of Carl Ludwig Engel in Helsinki and many simple vernacular structures in the countryside. On the ceiling, a bare light bulb is set in a commercially produced stamped brass fixture. The vestibule leads to a sink, water closet, and small storage room, as well as through an oak-paneled door to a covered walkway that strategically connected Eliel's studio with the studio used by his students in the architecture department. Louis Redstone, one of the students who studied urban planning under Eliel in the 1940s, recalled the significance of this passage:

> Saarinen, whose studio and residence was across the narrow landscaped walkway from the architectural drafting room, would visit during the day or evening (work never ceased there).... All of us hesitated to visit him at his studio, apprehensive that we might interfere with his work. One afternoon I took courage and knocked at his door. To my pleasant surprise he received me with open arms, served me a drink, and asked

Figure 30
Saarinen House, Studio and Studio Office, during a party, with Marianne Strengell, head of the Department of Weaving and Textile Design (far left). ca. 1940s

whether I was interested in hearing excerpts from the manuscript of his forthcoming book. Only then did I realize how pleased he was to have students visit.[150]

Redstone recalls many subsequent conversations with Eliel, but his Saarinen House visits were limited to the studio. Only on special occasions such as the annual student teas did Eliel and Loja open the living and dining room to students.[151]

The Second Floor Hallway

Like the studio vestibule, the front stairway and second floor hallway demonstrate Eliel's skill as a colorist (see fig. 9). At the bottom of the steps, the wall color changes almost imperceptibly from the warm soft gold in the entrance hall to the cool gray green used on the walls and ceiling in the hallway. A much darker green is used on the door jambs and back moldings, and a third green is used on the doors themselves. A fourth paint color, a medium brown, is used on the cap molding, forming a transition between the dark stained oak base moldings and the painted walls. Likewise, a transition occurs in the balusters, which are stained on the first floor but painted in the second floor hallway. This change, however, does not occur at the second floor level but rather above the base and cap molding, strengthening the impression that the balusters are single lengths of wood that pierce the floor before terminating as supports for the second floor hallway railing. Eliel's panache again is evident inside the closets, where he contrasts the subdued palette of the hall with bright turquoise walls and blue green shelves.

Based on the research of the historic-paint consultant Frank Welsh, we know that most of the spaces in the house were initially painted a light tan. After Eliel and Loja had lived in the house for a period of time, as indicated by a film of dirt on top of this paint layer, the spaces were repainted in a much richer and more complex color scheme, an example of which was in the hallway, as described above. The second color scheme, rather than the first, was used

in the restoration. Perhaps because the house was first painted under the supervision of J. Robert F. Swanson while Eliel and Loja were in Europe, the interior was painted a uniform color to insure that it would be ready for the Saarinens upon their return in September. This allowed Eliel to determine the final color scheme after the furnishings were installed and he and Loja had lived in the spaces.

A careful examination of the historic photograph of the second floor hallway showing the closed closet and bedroom doors reveals that there were painted or stenciled designs located at eye level on the front of all the hallway doors. While a decorative detail such as this is incongruous with twentieth-century modernism, it continues the Finnish tradition of figurative decoration that Eliel employed throughout his buildings in his native country. Later residents stripped these designs from the doors, leaving us just the one grainy photograph as evidence of this important detail. Although historic photographs were used successfully to guide other aspects of the restoration, enlargements of this detail did not provide sufficient information and it was necessary to use evidence found in other buildings Saarinen designed both to identify the artist and to re-create the motif in the hallway.

Eight years after Saarinen House was finished, Eliel, Eero, and Robert Swanson completed a residence in Grosse Pointe Farms, Michigan, for Charles and Ingrid Koebel, a home which resembles Saarinen House in many respects. On each of the doors in the second floor hallway, Pipsan painted a pattern consisting of two stylized flowers behind a superimposed chevron. While the documented designs in the Koebel house indicate Pipsan was also responsible for the designs in Saarinen House, their overall form is more geometric than those that appear in the historic photograph; as a result, they were not used as patterns for the designs in Saarinen House. The patterns used in the restoration came from designs that Pipsan painted on the

shutters of the second floor dining room in Kingswood School for girls. As Pipsan created these designs about the same time that Saarinen House was completed, and their round overall form approximates the pattern in the photograph, their use in the current restoration seemed appropriate.

Like the living room and studio, the second floor hallway has an alcove at the south end outside the master bedroom (fig. 31). It is furnished with a long bench, an armchair, and a table, and is the space where Anna Danielson served the Saarinens' breakfast each morning. The alcoves are the most personal spaces in the house. While their intimacy is established by the architecture itself, the detailing of the furniture and textiles creates their warmth. More than anywhere else in the house, the detailing in this alcove comes directly from Scandinavia. The bench and table are reminiscent of eighteenth-century Gustavian furniture from Sweden, and the geometric pattern in Loja's curtain reflects the motifs found on textiles from Karelia, the region of present-day Russia bordering Finland, whose buildings and ornamentation were an important inspiration for the development of Finland's "indigenous" building style at the turn of the century. Like the curtains in the book room, this curtain has a translucence that softens but does not block the view toward the street. The transition is further accomplished by the triangular pattern in the

leaded glass windows, a pattern which is complemented by the geometric pattern woven in the curtains. On the floor are cotton rag rugs with geometric inlays, perhaps abstracted houses, which have a long tradition in Finland although they are rarely used so prominently in an American house of this size and expense. Two more antique Finnish *ryijy* rugs hung in the stairway during the Saarinens' residency, although just one has been included in the restoration.[152]

The Master Bedroom

The master bedroom is the single room in the house where Eliel's role as an interior designer was completely subordinated (fig. 32). The furniture was designed by Eero, who at the time was barely twenty years old. For his auspicious debut as a furniture designer, he created a suite of wood furniture, including a table, twin beds, a night stand, and a dressing-table bench, painted to match the gray-green wall color. The furniture is distinguished from Eliel's designs throughout the house by their *moderne* streamlined curves. The curved detailing introduced by this set would become a leitmotif of Eero's work as an architect, from early projects such as the Kleinhans Music Hall in Buffalo (1938–40),

Figure 31
Saarinen House, Second Floor Hallway Seating Alcove. Photographed ca. September 1930

Figure 32
Saarinen House, Master Bedroom. Photographed ca. 1930

Figure 33
Saarinen House, Master
Bedroom, Dressing Table.
Photographed ca. 1930

Figure 34
Hvitträsk, Bedroom in the
North Wing. Photographed
probably after 1916

where he collaborated with his father, to his own mature works, including the Trans World Airlines Terminal in New York (1956–62).

Tor Berglund received the order to make the twin beds for the master bedroom on July 17, 1930, a fact noted in the ledger kept by the Cranbrook Foundation on the craft shops at Cranbrook Academy of Art.[153] Although they are also noted on the inventory of furnishings that Loja prepared in 1950, they, like the lounge chair in the master bedroom and the upholstered benches in the front entrance hall, have disappeared. Whereas the lounge chair and bench at least are documented by historic black and white photographs, no photographs showing the beds have been located. The beds used in the current restoration, therefore, are interpretations based on the evidence suggested by the surviving furniture and the architectural detailing of the room itself. Likewise, the bedspreads are interpretations based on Loja's note, "2 bedspreads, taffeta," in her 1950 inventory and the memories of Anna Danielson, who recalls that they were "tan" with "gathered ruffles" dropping down the sides.[154]

The focal point of the master bedroom is the rose, yellow, and light green upholstery used on the banquette, the lounge chair, and dressing table bench. Although the selvage of the upholstery indicates the material was not woven by hand at Cranbrook, the assumption is that Loja designed the material in collaboration with a commercial mill. The chevron pattern continues the triangular theme established by Eliel in the leaded glass windows, while the rose color is a perfect complement to the gray-green walls. On the floor are two more cotton rag rugs, the largest of which is documented as a design of Maja Andersson Wirde, Loja's chief assistant in Studio Loja Saarinen.[155] Like that on the upholstery, the pattern on the rugs is another variation of the triangular motif. The textiles in the room are completed with white voile curtains and an elaborate pair of voile side panels with a valance framing the dressing table (fig. 33). To modern sensibilities, the voile curtains with their black piping on the edge of the ruffles may strike a dissonant chord. In the context of the period, however, an era remembered for its flapper dresses, among other designs, the curtains are quite contemporary. An additional precedent are the curtains and lamp shade the Saarinens used in one of the bedrooms at Hvitträsk (fig. 34).

Eliel's distance from the design of this room is also evident in the pictures that hang on the walls. The room contained five portraits, all of which depict Loja's German-Finnish ancestors. The only documented portrait in the house depicting one of Eliel's relatives is the portrait of his father that initially hung in the cozy corner off the studio. Anna Danielson has suggested that Loja was the person "in charge" of the private spaces of the house and that Eliel was content to be able to control the studio. It is impor-

However, no documentation has been found in the archives of Cranbrook or the pottery to support this attribution, and recent documentation suggests that the same commercial tile employed elsewhere in the house was installed in the master bathroom. Nevertheless, the room remains a remarkable example of Eliel's ability to use architecture to celebrate life's daily rituals.

The Bedrooms

The upstairs includes four additional bedrooms, for which little documentation exists. The bedroom adjacent to the master bedroom, the only other bedroom included in the current restoration, is variously labeled "Bedroom #2" or "Son's Bedroom" on the architectural drawings, although Eliel and Loja referred to it, of course, as "Eero's room." We know that Eero designed a bed for this room that was made by Berglund,[158] but we cannot document any other furnishings. In her 1950 inventory of the house, Loja referred to it as the "Blue Room." Recent paint analysis has confirmed that a later layer of paint indeed was blue. The woodwork in the room is gum and was originally finished with a combination of graining and orange shellac varnish.[159] The painting specifications also note that one of the bedrooms, probably this one, was to have Fabricoid, or jute cloth, on the walls, the same cloth that was used in 1930 in the living room.[160] The Saarinens called the next bedroom, "Bedroom #3," the "Guest Room." They furnished it with the furniture and textiles from the "Room for a Lady" Eliel designed for the 1934 exhibition *Contemporary Industrial Art* at the Metropolitan Museum of Art (fig. 36).[161] "Bedroom #4" was used during the 1930s as a sewing room, and the final room, "Bedroom #5," was the maid's room. The maid's room did not have a door leading to the second floor hallway but rather was entered through the sewing room or the back stairway that connected it with the kitchen on the first floor. A second bathroom, similar in detailing to the master bathroom but less grand, is located at the top of the front stairway, and a third one is located off the maid's room.

Figure 35
Saarinen House, Master Bathroom. Photographed ca. September 1930

tant to consider the individual personalities of Eliel and Loja. Henry Booth described the couple in the following manner: "Mrs. Saarinen you must know, was a retiring person, Mr. Saarinen was much less formal. And he had a real sense of humor. I think Mrs. Saarinen must have had a sense of humor but she never relaxed in the same way that he did."[156] Perhaps Loja was not only responsible for defining the aesthetics of the master bedroom, but her personality also determined the formality of the living room.

The master bathroom is one of the most dramatic spaces in the house (fig. 35). Entered through one of the three mirrored doors on the east wall of the bedroom—mirrors that seem to negate the possibility of another space beyond the wall—the axis of the bedroom cuts across the width of the bathroom and culminates in the bathtub, recessed like an altar. To the left and right, at opposite ends of the length of the bathroom, are lavatories with custom designed basins set in counters of yellow Vitrolite glass.[157] Centered above each of the lavatories is a mirror with two windows on either side, an arrangement that permits natural light to illuminate the face when standing in front of the mirror. A curtained water closet and shower stall with a bidet complete the plan. The room's drama is achieved through the use of tan and black ceramic tile arranged in a grid on the floor and walls. For many years the tile was believed to have been made by the Pewabic Pottery under the direction of Mary Chase Perry Stratton.

Figure 36

"Room for a Lady" by Eliel
Saarinen, installed in the
*Exhibition of Home
Furnishings,* Cranbrook
Pavilion, May 12–27, 1935.
Photographed May 1935

At some point, the guest room and the sewing room were combined into one large space. The door leading from the hallway to the sewing room was retained, and the door that originally led to the guest room became a closet off the second floor hallway. The possibility that this was done under Eliel's supervision is suggested by the consistency of the architectural detailing maintained in the enlarged room and new closet, as well as the fact that Loja notes just four rooms, the master bedroom, blue room, guest room, and maid's room, in her 1950 inventory.[162] Anna Danielson, however, recalls that there remained five separate bedrooms while the Saarinens lived in the house.

SAARINEN HOUSE AFTER 1950

Eliel Saarinen's tenure at Cranbrook and residency in Saarinen House ended with his death on July 1, 1950. As Christ-Janer recounts, Loja was reading aloud a letter from their friend the Finnish composer Jean Sibelius while Eliel sat in Eero's "womb" chair, which had replaced the lounge chair in the master bedroom: "Sibelius wrote, 'many hearty thanks for the cigars. When I smoke them the memories of the sparkling parties of Hvitträsk, which Aino and I so thoroughly enjoyed, come back in strong colors.' When Loja had finished reading, she turned to Eliel, for he had not answered. His face was serene."[163] On July 5 a memorial service was held for Saarinen at Christ Church Cranbrook and on July 21, after a memorial service at the University of Helsinki attended by Loja and Eero, his ashes were taken to Hvitträsk for burial.[164] Eliel's long and prodigious career, one that spanned two continents and influenced over fifty years of modern design, had come to an end, and with it the first chapter of the life of Saarinen House.

Loja remained in the house for over a year, in part to more easily help plan the retrospective of Eliel's work that took place in April and May of 1951 at the academy art museum. At the same time Eero was designing a new home for his mother, behind his own home on Vaughn Road, less than a mile from Saarinen House. On September 13, 1951, she wrote a letter to Henry Booth, president of the Cranbrook Foundation:

> May I once more express my gratitude for the Academy's great hospitality.
>
> It meant so much to me to be able to stay at Cranbrook, where I could help Miss Gatling with the Memorial Exhibition and where I had space enough to wind up Eliel's residue and finally pack and move my own things. I hardly could have accomplished that if I first had to move into a small apartment. It is amazing how much one can accumulate in twenty-five years of time!
>
> I am deeply grateful that you let me stay on.
>
> In about two weeks I hope to have my little house in order and hope that you and Mrs. Booth will come over and see my new home.[165]

The home Eero designed for Loja—a glass and plywood box in the manner of Ludwig Mies van der Rohe's Farnsworth House in Plano, Illinois (1945–50), and the Glass House, Philip Johnson's home in New Canaan, Connecticut (1949)—symbolizes the next chapter in the history of Saarinen House. During the 1950s and 1960s, the International Style was the only respected branch of modernism, and the subsequent residents of Saarinen House each made changes to it that reflected new fashions. Shortly after Loja moved out of the house, Sepeshy, who directed the academy from 1946 to 1966, and his family began their residence. A photograph dated November 26, 1951, shows their newly refinished floors in the living room and dining room, now a light brown rather than the deep black stain that was a stunning background for Loja's rugs.[166] Times had changed and even Loja had her son-in-law's bar buffet refinished, bleaching the original green brown stain, which remains on the credenza Eliel used in the studio, to obtain the light finish found on the bar buffet today.[167]

The Sepeshys were followed by the third president, Glen Paulsen, an architect, who with his wife and daughter lived in the house from July 1966 through May 1970. Upon their arrival the Paulsens found a studio that already had been divided into three distinct spaces, including an enclosed studio alcove and a faculty room in the former office alcove at the east end. Among other changes that had already been made were the removal of the mirror in the entrance hall and the addition of acoustical tile on the ceiling in the second floor hallway. Faced with worn surfaces and a limited budget for restoration, Paulsen removed the soiled jute-cloth in the living room and asked the maintenance staff to cover the paneling in the dining room with new wallboard. He admits he was surprised to learn that the workers had removed the paneling.[168] The Paulsens were followed by Wallace Mitchell, a painter who served as the academy's fourth president from 1970 until his death in January 1977. By this time, the accumulation of many changes—each carefully justified at the time—had produced a house that bore little resemblance to the "beautiful and unified whole" Florence Davies described in September 1930.[169] When Roy Slade arrived in 1977, he had the opportunity to meet Pipsan Saarinen Swanson and demonstrate his commitment to restore Saarinen House to her parents' original intent. Before she died the following year, she had returned to Cranbrook many original objects from the house, a legacy which continues today through the encouragement and generous

Figure 37

Saarinen House, Courtyard,
with Eliel and Loja Saarinen.
Photographed early 1940s

support of her sons, Robert Saarinen Swanson and Ronald Saarinen Swanson.

Alvar Aalto described fellow countryman Eliel Saarinen as a "bridge builder," an architect who was able to connect his architectural heritage with contemporary forms of expression.[170] This statement also defines the significance of Saarinen House. Drawing upon both the rich traditions of the Arts and Crafts movement, as exemplified by the integrated interior and exterior of Hvitträsk, and the tenets of modernism as it developed in the 1920s, Eliel and Loja Saarinen (fig. 37) designed a home at Cranbrook that was dynamic in its plan, clear in its use of ornament and detail, and precise in its selection and arrangement of furnishings— an alternative modernism. In 1936 Kenneth Reid wrote: "Saarinen is neither a radical thinker nor a conservative thinker—just a rather straight thinker who considers poetry at least as important as prose; beauty in design as much to be sought after as functional perfection. And to follow the quest for beautiful and appropriate form he regards as the duty of all of us."[171] These seemingly modest aims created a home of enduring beauty: a total work of art.

Plate 1

Front Entrance in autumn

A WALK THROUGH SAARINEN HOUSE AND GARDEN

Photography by Balthazar Korab

**Catalogue of the Saarinen House Collection
by Gregory Wittkopp with David D. J. Rau**

Unless otherwise noted, all objects listed were originally produced or acquired for the house in the United States under the direction of Eliel and Loja Saarinen and are in the collection of Cranbrook Academy of Art Museum. The term "reproduction" means that the object is not original but a faithful copy of the original. The term "adaptation" means that the object is in the spirit of the original but modified for various reasons. All dimensions are in inches; height precedes width precedes depth.

Plate 2

- *Saarinen House Entrance Plaque*
  Designed by Henry Booth, made early 1950s
  Carved limestone,
  8 ¼ x 20 ¹⁄₁₆ in.

Plate 3

Front Entrance in late
spring with Father Hugo
roses in bloom

Plate 4
Milles House
and Saarinen House (right)
on Academy Way

Plate 5
Saarinen House in autumn

Plate 6
Side Garden and Walkway
in late summer

Plate 7
Front Garden in late spring,
view from Side Garden

Plate 8
Saarinen House (center) in
winter, view from Cranbrook
School for boys

Plate 9
Saarinen House in winter

Plate 11

Front Entrance Hall, view from Living Room

- *Reproduction Living Room/Front Entrance Hall Portières*

  Original design attributed to Loja Saarinen, ca. 1930; reproductions made by Rita Grendze and Kate Humphrey, 1993

  Reproduction gray striped and adaptation gold cotton velvet fabrics; two panels, each 102 x 35 in.

- *Reproduction Gray Striped Fabric for Portières*

  Reproduction designed by Christine Walsh and woven by Collins and Aikman Corporation, 1993

  Voided cotton and rayon velvet, bolt width 57 in.

  Gift of Collins and Aikman Corporation, 1994.2

- *Adaptation Gold Fabric for Portières*

  Produced by J. H. Thorp and Company, Inc., ca. 1993

  Cotton velvet

Plate 12

Front Entrance Hall, view from Living Room

- *Reproduction Rug*

  Original design attributed to Loja Saarinen and weaving attributed to Studio Loja Saarinen, ca. 1930–31; reproduction designed by Celeste Brush and woven by Christina Bechstein and Celeste Brush, 1993–94

  Linen warp, wool weft; weft-faced tapestry weave, 82 x 71 in.; with fringe, 95 x 71 in.

  1994.4

Plate 10

Saarinen House in early spring with star magnolia in bloom

Plate 13
Living Room, view from Front
Entrance Hall

Plate 14

Front Entrance Hall, view from Coat Room

- *Table*

  Designed by Eliel Saarinen and made by Tor Berglund, 1930

  Wood frame with rosewood or Macassar ebony and other wood veneers, each 16 ⅛ x 30 x 12 ½ in.

  1977.4

- *Reproduction Benches*

  Originals designed by Eliel Saarinen and made by Tor Berglund, 1930; reproductions made by Charles Phipps and Sons, Ltd., under the direction of Charles Phipps, 1993

  Maple frame with Macassar ebony veneers, light Honduras mahogany inlays, and maple stringing; two benches, each 16 ⅛ x 25 x 16 in.

  1993.39–.40

- *Adaptation Upholstery for Reproduction Benches*

  Original design attributed to Loja Saarinen and weaving attributed to Studio Loja Saarinen, ca. 1930; adaptation designed by Paula Stebbins Becker and woven by Craftex Mills, Inc. of Penna., 1993

  Rayon warp, rayon weft with cotton and rayon chenille; Jacquard weave, bolt width 56 in.

  Gift of Craftex Mills, Inc. of Penna., 1994.3

Plate 15

Front Entrance Hall, view of Ceiling Lights

Plate 17
Front Entrance Hall, view
toward Coat Room

- *Reproduction Wall Light
  Fixture*
  Original design by Eliel
  Saarinen, 1930; reproduc-
  tion made by David Kostich,
  1991–92

Fabricated bronze with
copper, 8 ½ x 5 x 5 ⅜ in.
1994.5

- *Adaptation Front Entrance
  Hall/Coat Room Portières*
  Adaptations made by
  Marianne McCann, 1994
  Adaptation gold cotton
  velvet fabric; two panels,
  each 87 x 24 in.

Plate 18
Front Entrance Hall, view
from Second Floor Hallway

Plate 16
Living Room, view from Front
Entrance Hall

- *Sofa Ends*
  Designed by Eliel Saarinen
  and made by Tor Berglund,
  1930
  Wood frame with greenhart,
  African walnut, rosewood,
  and maple veneers; two ends,
  each 21 ⅞ x 29 ¹⁵⁄₁₆ x 8 ⁷⁄₁₆ in.
  1972.15–.16

- *Sofa Cover*
  Designed by Loja Saarinen
  and woven by Studio Loja
  Saarinen, ca. 1929–30
  Linen warp, wool weft, wool
  pile; plain weave with *ryijy-*
  knotted pile, 96 x 68 in.
  ZO 1978 8

- *Reproduction Pillow*
  Original design attributed to
  Loja Saarinen, ca. 1930;
  reproduction made by Kimon
  Florias, 1993
  Cotton velvet cover, cotton
  liner, and feather stuffing,
  22 x 22 in.

- *Photograph of "Girl in Rocking
  Chair"*
  Original drawn by Helene
  Schjerfbeck, Finland, 1910;
  photograph printed 1993
  Original materials: gouache,
  charcoal, and pencil on
  paper; framed, 32 ½ x
  24 ⅜ in.
  Original drawing formerly in
  the collection of Eliel and
  Loja Saarinen, presently in
  the collection of Rauno
  Puolimatka, Finland.
  Reproduction courtesy
  of Rauno Puolimatka and
  Carl Appelberg

Plate 19

Living Room

- *Fireplace Mantel*

  Designed by Eliel Saarinen
  and made by Pewabic Pottery
  under the direction of Mary
  Chase Perry Stratton,
  1928–29; installed 1930

  Glazed ceramic tile, 116 ¾ x
  47 ¾ x 5 ¼ in.

  Gift of Mary Chase Perry
  Stratton

- *Torchères*

  Designed by Eliel Saarinen
  and made by Edward F.
  Caldwell and Company, Inc.,
  1930

  Cast bronze bases, spun and
  hammered copper shades,
  both patinated; three
  torchères, each 68 ¼ x
  14 ¼ in.

  1972.24–.26

- *Wall Hanging*

  Designed by Loja Saarinen
  and woven by Studio Loja
  Saarinen, ca. 1929–30

Linen warp, wool weft, synthetic cellulose fiber
"Lustrone" pile (viscose
rayon); plain weave with *ryijy*-
knotted pile, excluding
reproduction fringe,
50 x 51 in.

Gift of Virginia Christ-Janer,
ZO 1980 37

- *Peacock Andirons*

  Designed by Eliel Saarinen
  and produced by Sterling
  Bronze Company, 1928–29

  Cast bronze, each 22 ⅜ x
  21 ¼ x 27 ¼ in.

  1985.2 a–b

- *Ewer* (not pictured)

  Made in Europe, probably
  nineteenth century

  Fabricated brass, 15 ½ x
  12 ¾ x 9 ¾ in.

  Collection of Ronald
  Saarinen Swanson

- *Adaptation Wall Covering*

  Produced by Bradbury and
  Bradbury Art Wallpapers,
  1993

  Dyed jute and cotton on
  paper, roll width 35 in.

Plate 21
Living Room Rug by Loja
Saarinen, detail (see plate 20)

Plate 20

Living Room, view from
Dining Room

- *Living Room Armchairs*

  Designed by Eliel Saarinen
  and made by Tor Berglund,
  1929–30

  Wood frame with greenhart,
  African walnut, rosewood,
  and maple veneers; two with
  original upholstery and two
  with reproduction upholstery,
  each 30 ¾ x 22 x 25 ½ in.

  1972.12, .13, .29, and .30

- *Armchair Upholstery*

  Designed by Loja Saarinen
  and woven by Gerda Nyberg
  for Studio Loja Saarinen,
  1929–30

  Linen and silk; plain weave
  ground with supplementary
  wefts; handwoven

- *Reproduction Upholstery for
  Living Room Armchairs and
  Book Room Lounge Chairs*

  Reproduction designed by
  Unika Vaev USA, 1984–86,
  and produced by Unika Vaev
  USA, 1992

  Rayon; Jacquard weave, bolt
  width 55 in.

  Gift of Unika Vaev
  USA/International Contract
  Furnishings Inc., 1994.21

- *Living Room Rug*

  Designed by Loja Saarinen
  and woven by Studio Loja
  Saarinen, ca. 1929–30

  Linen warp, wool weft, wool
  pile; plain weave with *ryijy*-
  knotted pile, 228 x 73 in.

  1973.21

- *Side Chairs* (not pictured)

  Design attributed to Eero
  Saarinen, ca. 1929–31;
  production possibly by
  Ypsilanti Reed Furniture
  Company, ca. 1929–31

  Painted tubular steel, caning;
  two chairs, each 31 ⅞ x
  16 ⅜ x 21 in.

  1994.34–.35

Plate 22
Torchère by Eliel Saarinen,
detail (see plate 19)

Plate 23
Armchair by Eliel Saarinen, detail (see plate 20)

Plate 24
Peacock Andiron by Eliel Saarinen (see plate 19)

Plate 25
▪ *Aztec-style Figure*
Carved in Mexico, after mid-nineteenth century
Volcanic stone, 7 x 3 ¼ x 2 ½ in.
Collection of Ronald Saarinen Swanson

Plate 27

Portrait of Loja Saarinen by
Eliel Saarinen, detail
(see plate 26)

Plate 26

Living Room and Book Room,
view from Dining Room

▪ *Cabinet or Bookcase*

Designed by Eliel Saarinen
and made by Tor Berglund,
1929–30

Wood frame with greenhart,
African walnut, rosewood,
maple, birch, burl, and
mahogany veneers, 39 ⁵/₈ x
60 x 15 in.

1972.17

▪ *Portrait of Loja Saarinen*

Painted by Eliel Saarinen,
Finland, 1922

Oil on canvas, original frame
with mahogany veneers; canvas, 24 ¼ x 17 ³/₁₆ in.; frame,
31 ³/₈ x 24 x ³/₁₆ in.

Gift of Ronald Saarinen
Swanson, 1994.46

Plate 28

▪ *Cranbrook Academy of Art
Guest Book*

Designed and made by
Jean Eschmann, 1932

Gilded leather and paper,
10 ⁵/₁₆ x 7 ¹⁵/₁₆ x ⁷/₈ in.

Collection of Robert
Saarinen Swanson and
Ronald Saarinen Swanson

Plate 29
Cabinet or Bookcase
 by Eliel Saarinen, detail of
door interior
(see plate 26)

Plate 30

Book Room

▪ *Cigarette Box and Ashtray*

Made in Germany, before
ca. 1942

Fabricated sterling silver with
wood interior; cigarette box,
1½ x 5 ⁵⁄₁₆ x 3 ¹³⁄₁₆ in.; ashtray,
1½ x 3 ⅛ x 3 ⅛ in.

Collection of Ronald
Saarinen Swanson

Plate 31

Book Room

- *Book Room Table*

  Designed by Eliel Saarinen and made by Tor Berglund, ca. 1929–30

  Wood frame with greenhart, African walnut, rosewood, and maple veneers, 26 1/16 x 30 1/16 x 30 1/16 in.

  1982.51

- *Book Room Lounge Chairs*

  Designed by Eliel Saarinen and made by Tor Berglund, 1929–30

  Wood frame with greenhart, African walnut, ebony, rosewood, and maple veneers with reproduction upholstery; two chairs, each 35 x 34 x 32 in.

  1972.10–.11

- *Hanging Lamp*

  Designed by Eliel Saarinen and produced by Edward F. Caldwell and Company, Inc., ca. 1930–31

  Spun and hammered copper shade, lathe-turned brass hangers, all patinated, 52 1/4 x 17 in.

  1994.22

- *Book Room Rug*

  Designed by Loja Saarinen and woven by Gerda Nyberg and Elizabeth Edmark for Studio Loja Saarinen, ca. 1930–31

  Linen warp, wool weft, wool pile; plain weave with *ryijy*-knotted pile, 145 x 102 in.

  ZO 1978 7

- *Collection of Eliel and Loja Saarinen's Books*

  Gift of Robert Saarinen Swanson and Ronald Saarinen Swanson

Plate 32
Lounge Chair with
Reproduction Upholstery,
detail (see plates 20, 31)

Plate 33
Book Room, view of
Reproduction Curtain with
objects on window ledge

▪ *Reproduction Curtains*
Original design by Loja
Saarinen, woven by Studio
Loja Saarinen, ca. 1930–31;
reproduction designed by
Paula Stebbins Becker,
woven by Paula Stebbins

Becker assisted by Kristen
Dettoni, and hemmed by
Paula Stebbins Becker and
Lori Calentine, 1993, with
yarns dyed by Globe Dye
Works Company

Wet-spun linen warp with
wool stripe, wet-spun linen
weft; plain weave, two panels,
each 73 x 80 in.

1994.6 a–b

Plate 34

▪ *"Hirvenvasa" ("Elk")*
(see plate 33)

Sculpted by Jussi Mäntynen
and cast in Finland, 1928

Cast bronze, 11 ½ x 6 x 5 ½ in.

Collection of Ronald
Saarinen Swanson

Plate 35

- *Primavera Vase* (see plate 33)

Produced by Atelier Primavera, Les Grands Magasins du Printemps, Paris, France, ca. 1930s

Glazed ceramic, 17 3/8 x 5 5/8 in.

Collection of Robert Saarinen Swanson

Plate 36

- *"Young Pegasus"* (see plate 33)

Sculpted by Viktor Schreckengost and fired at the Cleveland Institute of Art, 1937

Red clay with raw borax glaze, 11 1/2 x 9 x 4 in.

Collection of Robert Saarinen Swanson and Ronald Saarinen Swanson

Plate 39
Book Room, view out window
in late spring with weigela
in bloom

Plate 37
- *Tree of Life* (see plate 33)
  Sculpted by Lili Markus,
  Hungary, ca. 1930s
  Glazed ceramic, 26 ½ x 14 ½
  x 6 ½ in.
  Collection of Robert
  Saarinen Swanson

Plate 38
- *Head and Torso of a Young
  Woman* (see plate 33)
  Sculpted by Rudolf Knörlein,
  Austria, ca. 1930s
  Glazed ceramic, 19 x 9 ½
  x 6 in.
  Gift of Pat and
  E. Jan Hartmann, 1993.20

Plate 41

Living Room

▪ *Globe Stand*

Designed by J. Robert F.
Swanson and made by
Tor Berglund, ca. 1931–32

Wood frame with rosewood
or Macassar ebony veneers,
stainless steel, and globe,
50 ½ x 28 ½ x 20 in.

Gift of Robert Saarinen
Swanson and Ronald
Saarinen Swanson, 1993.5

Plate 42

▪ *"Sea Princess" from the Opera
"Sadko"* (see plate 40)

Sculpted by Mikhail Vrubel,
Russia, ca. 1889–1900

Glazed ceramic,
15 ⅝ x 9 ⅜ x 5 ⅛ in.

Gift of Pipsan Saarinen
Swanson and J. Robert F.
Swanson, 1979.4

Plate 40

Living Room and Dining
Room, view from Book Room

▪ *Sculpture Pedestal*

Designed by Eliel Saarinen
and made by Tor Berglund,
1930

Wood frame with rosewood
or Macassar ebony veneers,
48 ⅜ x 9 ¹⁵⁄₁₆ x 7 ⁷⁄₁₆ in.

Collection of Ronald
Saarinen Swanson

▪ *Reproduction Living
Room/Dining Room Portières*

Original design attributed to
Loja Saarinen, ca. 1930;
reproductions made by
Marianne McCann assisted
by Becky Hart, 1993–94

Reproduction gray striped
cotton velvet fabric and
reproduction linen and rayon
Dining Room Side Curtain
Panel fabric; two panels, each
101 x 60 in.

Plate 43

Dining Room, view from Pantry

- *Dining Room Table*

  Designed by Eliel Saarinen, 1929, and made by The Company of Master Craftsmen, 1930

  Wood frame with fir, ebony, hare holly, and boxwood veneers; with one of two sets of four leaves, 30 x 62 ¾ in.

  1972.19 a–i

- *Dining Room Side Chairs*

  Designed by Eliel Saarinen, 1929, and made by The Company of Master Craftsmen, 1930

  Fir or maple with black and ocher paint; six chairs with original upholstery and eight with reproduction upholstery, each 37 ⅝ x 17 x 20 in.

  1972.20 a–n

- *Upholstery for Dining Room Chairs*

  Designed by Loja Saarinen, ca. 1930

  Horsehair and cotton; plain weave

- *Reproduction Upholstery for Dining Room Chairs*

  Reproduction designed by Unika Vaev USA, 1984–87,

and produced by Unika Vaev USA, ca. 1990

Horsehair and cotton; plain weave

Gift of Unika Vaev USA/International Contract Furnishings Inc.

- *Dining Room Rug*

  Designed by Eliel Saarinen and made by Barrymore Seamless Wiltons, Inc., ca. 1928

  Wool warp, cotton weft, wool pile; machine woven in five sections, 133 x 128 ½ in.

  1973.19

- *Adaptation Dining Room Rug* (not pictured)

  Adaptation designed and produced by Bentley Mills, Inc., 1990–91

  Wool pile, latex backing; computer-assisted "Chroma-Tech" injection-dyed pattern, 134 ½ x 130 in.

  Gift of Bentley Mills, Inc., 1994.43

- *Hanging Lamp*

  Designed by Eliel Saarinen and made by Edward F. Caldwell and Company, Inc., under the direction of Victor F. von Lossberg, 1930

  Spun and hammered brass shade, lathe-turned hangers, all gilded; 40 x 21 in.

  1972.27

Plate 44

Dining Room

- *Centerpiece: Stylized Bird*

  Design attributed to Franz Hagenauer and produced by Werkstätte Hagenauer Wien, Austria, ca. 1930s (before 1938)

  Silver-plated nickel silver, 10 ⅝ x 6 ¼ x 2 ½ in.

  Collection of Robert Saarinen Swanson

Plate 45
Dining Room

- *Adaptation Curtains*
Adaptations designed by
Paula Stebbins Becker,
woven by Paula Stebbins
Becker assisted by Kenneth
Becker, and hemmed by
Paula Stebbins Becker,

Christina Bechstein, and
Suzanne Lentz, 1993, with
yarns dyed by Globe Dye
Works Company
Wet-spun linen warp with
wool stripe, wet-spun linen
weft with wool stripe;
plain weave, two panels,
each 100 x 60 in.
1994.8 a–b

Plate 46
Dining Room, view of
Courtyard with *"Kivi's Muse"*
by Wäinö Aaltonen
(see plate 65)

Plate 47

Courtyard in winter, view
from Center Bedroom

Plate 48

Dining Room, view from Living Room

- *Platter*

  Made in Europe, probably nineteenth century

  Hammered nickel silver, 15 7/16 x 1 1/8 in.

  Collection of Ronald Saarinen Swanson

- *Large Long-Handled Pot*

  Made in Europe, probably nineteenth century

  Brass with tinned interior, cast-iron handle, 5 1/2 x 15 3/8 x 5 7/8 in.

Collection of Ronald Saarinen Swanson

- *Small Long-Handled Pot*

  Made in Europe, probably nineteenth century

  Brass with tinned interior, cast-iron handle, 4 1/4 x 11 1/2 x 3 7/8 in.

  Collection of Ronald Saarinen Swanson

- *"Lovers in the Snow"*

  Image designed by Suzuki Harunobu, late 1760s; printer unknown

  Woodcut on paper; image, 11 13/16 x 7 11/16 in.; frame, 14 9/16 x 10 9/16 in.

  Collection of Robert Saarinen Swanson

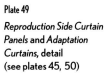

Plate 49

Reproduction Side Curtain Panels and *Adaptation Curtains*, detail (see plates 45, 50)

Plate 50

Dining Room, view of Corner Niche

- *Vase*

  Designed by Eliel Saarinen with production attributed to The Nessen Studio, Inc., or the International Silver Company, ca. 1935 (before September 1936)

  Spun brass bowl, fabricated brass base, 12 3/8 x 5 3/8 in.

  Gift of Peggy deSalle, 1977.8

- *Side Curtain Panels* (not pictured)

  Designed by Loja Saarinen and woven by Studio Loja Saarinen, ca. 1930

  Linen warp, rayon weft, two panels, each 97 1/2 x 27 1/2 in.

  1994.45 a–b

- *Reproduction Fabric for Side Curtain Panels*

  Reproduction designed by Paula Stebbins Becker, 1992–93, and woven by Paula Stebbins Becker assisted by Kristen Dettoni, 1993, with yarns dyed by Globe Dye Works Company

  Wet-spun linen warp, rayon weft; woven on a twenty-four harness computer-assisted AVL loom

  1994.7

- *Reproduction Side Curtain Panels*

  Originals designed by Loja Saarinen, ca. 1930; reproductions made by Paula Stebbins Becker, 1993

  Linen and rayon; two panels, each appx. 100 x 30 in.

Plate 51

Dining Room, view of
Corner Niche

- *Door Frames for Niches*

Designed by Eliel Saarinen
and supplied by Charles R.
Wermuth and Son, Inc., 1930

Cast bronze; four produced,
never installed, two extant,
each 58 ¼ x 19 ¾ x 1 ½ in.

1994.23.1–.2

Plate 52

Dining Room

- *Dinnerware*

Produced by Gefle

Black glazed stoneware;
eight dinner plates, 9 ⅝ in.;
eight salad plates, 7 ¼ in.;
platter, 13 ⁹⁄₁₆ in.

Collection of Robert
Saarinen Swanson

Plate 53
Dining Room, view of Dining
Room Table set for a tea

▪ *Wall Hanging: Landscape
with Tree and Birds*

Designed and woven
by Greta Skogster, Finland,
between 1935 and 1939

Linen, silk, cotton, wool,
and rayon; inlaid tapestry

weave, plain weave ground
with supplementary wefts,
83 ¾ x 126 ¾ in.

Gift of Pipsan Saarinen
Swanson and J. Robert F.
Swanson and Robert

Saarinen Swanson and
Ronald Saarinen Swanson
1979.7

Plate 54

Dining Room

▪ *Placemats*

Designed and printed by
Eero Saarinen, Finland,
ca. 1920

Linen warp, linen weft; plain
weave; block printed; six
placemats, each 12 in.

Gift of Ronald Saarinen
Swanson, 1988.55 a–f

Plate 55

Dining Room

▪ *Coffee Set*

Produced by Wiltshaw and
Robinson, Ltd., England,
after 1925

Glazed porcelain; coffee pot,
7 ⅝ x 3 ⅞ x 7 ¾ in.; creamer,
3 ⅛ x 2 ¾ x 3 ⅜ in.; sugar
bowl, 2 ¼ x 3 ¹¹⁄₁₆ in.; eight
cups, each 2 ³⁄₁₆ x 2 ¾ x 2 ¹⁄₁₆
in.; eight saucers, each ⅝
x 4 ⅛ in.

Collection of Robert
Saarinen Swanson

Plate 56

Dining Room

- *Glassware*

Produced by Orrefors Glasbruk, Sweden; design introduced 1939

Blown glass; twelve bowls, each 2 ¹³/₁₆ x 4 ⁵/₈ in.; six large-stemmed bowls, each 3 ¼ x 4 ⅛ in.; six small-stemmed bowls, each 4 x 3 ⅞ in.; seven wine glasses, each 4 ³/₈ x 2 ⁷/₈ in.; six water glasses, each 3 ¹⁵/₁₆ x 3 ³/₈ in.; six juice glasses, each 3 ¼ x 2 ¾ in.

Gift of Ronald Saarinen Swanson, 1994.24.1–.43

Plate 57

Dining Room

- *Decanter and Cordials*

Produced by Orrefors Glasbruk in Sweden; design introduced 1939

Blown glass; decanter, 10 x 3 ¹¹/₁₆ in.; six cordials, each 3 ¼ x 2 ³/₁₆ in.

Decanter in the collection of Ronald Saarinen Swanson

Cordials in the collection of Cranbrook Academy of Art Museum

Gift of Ronald Saarinen Swanson, 1994.24.44–.49

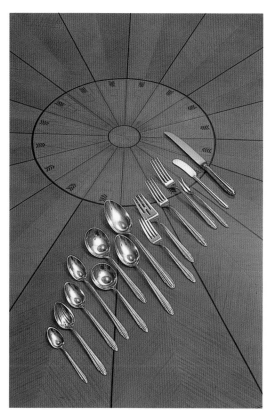

Plate 58

Dining Room

- *Selection of Flatware: "Contempora" Pattern*

  Designed by Eliel Saarinen, ca. 1927–28, for Dominick & Haff and produced by Dominick & Haff or Reed & Barton, ca. 1927–34

  Sterling silver; knife, 9 in.

  Collection of Nancy and Eric Saarinen

Plate 59

Dining Room

- *Creamer*

  Designed by Eliel Saarinen or Eero Saarinen and made by Antti Hakkarainen Taidetakomo, Finland, ca. 1935 (before September 1936)

  Spun nickel-silver, 2 x 5 3⁄8 x 3 15⁄16 in.

  Gift of Robert Saarinen Swanson and Ronald Saarinen Swanson, 1993.4

- *Creamer and Tray* (not pictured)

  Designed by Eliel Saarinen or Eero Saarinen and made by Antti Hakkarainen Taidetakomo, Finland, ca. 1935 (before September 1936)

  Spun nickel-silver; creamer, 1 15⁄16 x 5 11⁄16 x 4 in.; tray, 7⁄16 x 8 7⁄16 in.

  Collection of Ronald Saarinen Swanson

- *Sugar Bowl* (not pictured)

  Designed by Eliel Saarinen or Eero Saarinen and made by Svenskt Tenn, Sweden, ca. 1935 (before September 1936)

  Spun nickel-silver, 2 x 4 15⁄16 in.

  Collection of Ronald Saarinen Swanson

Plate 60

Dining Room

- *Coffeepot and Stand with Warmer*

  Designed by Eliel Saarinen and made in Finland, 1905–10

  Spun and fabricated brass; overall, 10 ½ x 9 x 6 ¾ in.; pot, 6 ¼ x 7 x 5 in.; stand, 4 ¼ x 6 ¾ x 6 ½ in.; burner, 3 ¼ x 3 ½ x 2 ¼ in.

  Collection of Ronald Saarinen Swanson

- *Creamer and Sugar Bowl*

  Designed by Jan Eisenlöffel and made in the Netherlands, ca. 1900

  Spun brass with wood knob; creamer, 2 ¼ x 3 ¹⁵⁄₁₆ x 2 ¹³⁄₁₆ in.; sugar bowl, 2 ⅞ x 5 ¾ x 4 ¼ in.

  Collection of Ronald Saarinen Swanson

- *Tray* (not pictured)

  Possibly made in Finland

  Spun brass, ⁹⁄₁₆ x 8 ½ in.

  Collection of Ronald Saarinen Swanson

- *Tray* (not pictured)

  Possibly made in Finland

  Spun brass, ⅝ x 18 ⅛ in.

  Collection of Ronald Saarinen Swanson

Plate 61

Dining Room

- *Coffee Urn and Tray*

  Designed by Eliel Saarinen and produced by the Wilcox Silver Plate Company/ International Silver Company, ca. 1933–34

  Spun and brass-plated nickel silver; urn, 14 ⅝ x 10 ⅞ in.; tray, ½ x 17 ½ in.

  Collection of Ronald Saarinen Swanson

- *Creamer and Sugar Bowl*

  Designed by Eliel Saarinen with production attributed to the Wilcox Silver Plate

Company/International Silver Company, ca. 1933–34, or Harry Bertoia, ca. 1938

Spun and brass-plated copper with tinned interiors; creamer, 3 x 3 ⅞ x 6 in.; sugar bowl, 6 ⅝ x 5 ⅞ x 3 ⅞ in.

Collection of Ronald Saarinen Swanson

- *Candy Plate* (not pictured)

  Designed by Eliel Saarinen and produced by The Nessen Studio, Inc., ca. 1935 (before September 1936)

  Spun brass, 5 ¹³⁄₁₆ x 8 ¹⁵⁄₁₆ in.

  Collection of Ronald Saarinen Swanson

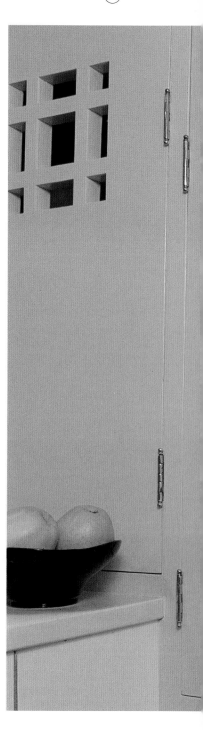

Plate 62

Pantry, view from
Dining Room

▪ *Bowl* (on refrigerator)
Glazed ceramic,
3 5/16 x 7 7/8 in.
Collection of Robert
Saarinen Swanson

Plate 63

Pantry, view from Coat Room

▪ *Dessert Plates* (not pictured)
Glass; eight plates, each
7 9/16 in.
Collection of Robert
Saarinen Swanson

Plate 64
Pantry, view of cabinets with tableware

Plate 65
Courtyard in late summer,
view from Dining Room

▪ *"Kiven Muusa" ("Kivi's Muse")*
from the *"Aleksis Kivi
Monument"*

Sculpted by Wäinö Aaltonen
and cast in Finland, designed
in 1926 and cast in 1930

Cast bronze, 54 x 30 ¾
x 34 ¾ in.

Gift of the Cranbrook
Foundation, 1930.29

Plate 66
Dining Room, Dome
with Hanging Lamp by
Eliel Saarinen (see plate 43)

Plate 67
Dining Room, view from
Courtyard

Plate 70

▪ *"Yllätetty yöjalkamies"* or *"Epätervetullut kosija"* *("Nightly Wooer Caught by Surprise"* or *"The Unwelcome Suitor")* (see plate 69)

Designed by Hannes Autere, 1925, and carved by Hannes Autere, Finland, 1926

Wood, 7 ⅞ x 10 ⅞ x 3 ⅛ in.

Collection of Ronald Saarinen Swanson

Plate 71

Studio Alcove, view of Doors to Courtyard

▪ *Leaded Glass Door Panel* (Lower Right Panel)

Designed by Eliel Saarinen and produced by Howie Glass Co., ca. 1930

Stained glass with leads; installed, 13 ¾ x 13 in.; overall, 14 ½ x 13 ½ in.

ZO 1978 5

▪ *Adaptation Leaded Glass Door Panels*

Original design by Eliel Saarinen, ca. 1930; adaptations produced and installed by Thompson Glass Co., 1979

Clear glass with leads; nineteen panels, installed, 13 x 13 in.; overall, 14 x 13 ½ in.

▪ *Runner*

Designed by Loja Saarinen and woven by Studio Loja Saarinen, ca. 1929–30

Linen warp, wool weft, wool pile; plain weave with *ryijy*-knotted pile, 123 x 47 in.

Gift of Patt Guido, 1993.48

Plate 69

Studio Alcove, view from Studio toward Living Room and Front Entrance Hall

▪ *Adaptation Green Fabric for Portières*

Produced by F. Schumacher and Company, ca. 1993

Cotton velvet

▪ *Reproduction Studio Alcove/Living Room Portières*

Original design attributed to Loja Saarinen, ca. 1930; reproductions made by Rita Grendze and Kate Humphrey, 1993

Adaptation green cotton velvet fabric and reproduction gray striped cotton velvet fabric; two panels, each 104 x 29 in.

Plate 68

Studio and Studio Alcove, view from Living Room

▪ *Smoking Table*

Designed by Eliel Saarinen and made by Tor Berglund, 1931

Wood frame with veneers, 21 x 27 ¾ x 27 ¾ in.

1972.18

▪ *Hanging Lamp*

Designed by Eliel Saarinen and produced by Edward F. Caldwell and Company, Inc., 1930

Spun and hammered copper shade, lathe-turned brass hangers, all patinated, 35 ¾ x 18 ¼ in.

1994.25

▪ *Adaptation Studio Alcove Rug*

Original designed by Loja Saarinen and woven by Studio Loja Saarinen, ca. 1929–30; adaptation woven by Tarja Heikkilä and Aila Mäkäräinen for The Friends of Finnish Handicraft, Finland, 1982

Linen warp, wool weft, wool pile; plain weave with *ryijy*-knotted pile, 104 x 98 in.

Original in the collection of the Finnish State

Adaptation in the collection of Cranbrook Academy of Art Museum

Gift of the Ministry of Education, Finland, ZO 1983 119

Plate 72
Studio Alcove, view from
Courtyard

Plate 73
Studio Alcove, view from
Courtyard

Plate 74
Studio Alcove
■ *Sketch for the "Sermon on the
Mount Hanging"*
Designed by Eliel Saarinen
and Loja Saarinen and drawn
by Eliel Saarinen, 1941
Pencil, colored pencil, and
gouache on paper; image,
26 ⅞ x 11 ¹³/₁₆ in.
Collection of Robert
Saarinen Swanson

Plate 75

Studio Alcove

- *Leaded Glass Windows*

 Designed by Eliel Saarinen,
 ca. 1930, and installed 1930

 Stained glass with leads, built
 in; three sections, each
 47 ¼ x 11 ½ in.

Plate 76

Studio Alcove

- *Vase from the "Dinanderie
 Collection"*

 Designed and produced
 by Christofle & Cie.,
 France, 1928

 Fabricated, copper-plated,
 then silver-plated brass,
 5 ⅜ x 4 ½ x 4 ½ in.

 Collection of Bertha Rowden

Plate 77

Studio Alcove, view from
Living Room

- *Bench Cover Fragments*
 (not pictured)

 Designed by Loja Saarinen
 and woven by Studio Loja
 Saarinen, ca. 1929–30

 Linen warp, wool weft, wool
 pile; plain weave with *ryijy*-
 knotted pile

 1973.22

- *Reproduction Bench Cover*

 Reproduction woven by Kay
 Dawson, 1983

 Linen warp, wool weft,
 wool pile; plain weave with
 ryijy-knotted pile, 43 x 123
 x 123 in.

 ZO 1983 122

- *Reproduction Pillows*

 Original design attributed to
 Loja Saarinen, ca. 1930;
 reproductions made by
 Kimon Florias, 1993

 Cotton velvet cover, cotton
 liner, and feather stuffing;
 twelve pillows, each
 22 x 22 in.

- *Pillow* (not pictured)

 Design attributed to Loja
 Saarinen, ca. 1930; made
 ca. 1930

 Cotton velvet cover, cotton
 liner, and feather stuffing,
 21 ½ x 17 ½ in.

 Collection of Ronald
 Saarinen Swanson

- *Boy Doll*

 Designed by Käthe Kruse
 and produced by Käthe
 Kruse Puppen GmbH,
 Germany, ca. 1910–20

 Molded muslin body with
 painted features, hair, and
 original clothes; jointed body,
 overall length 16 ¾ in.

 Gift of Ronald Saarinen
 Swanson, 1994.48

- *"Lenci" Girl Doll*

 Produced by Enrico and
 Elenadi, Italy, ca. 1920

 Pressed felt body with
 painted features, mohair hair,
 and original clothes; jointed
 body, overall length 17 in.

 Gift of Ronald Saarinen
 Swanson, 1994.47

Plate 79
Hanging Lamp by
Eliel Saarinen,
detail (see plate 68)

Plate 78
Studio Alcove

• *Ash Bowl*
  Produced in Czechoslovakia,
  after 1921
  Glass, 2 7/16 x 5 in.
  Collection of Ronald
  Saarinen Swanson

• *"Argenta Ware" Decanter*
  Designed by Wilhelm Kåge
  and produced by A. B.
  Gustavsberg, Sweden, 1931
  Stoneware with silver,
  7 13/16 x 3 1/2 in.
  Collection of Robert
  Saarinen Swanson

Plate 80

- *Still Life with Flowers*
  (see plate 77)

  Painted by Wallace Mitchell,
  1938

  Oil on board, adaptation
  frame; board, 24 x 18 in.

  Gift of Peggy deSalle,
  1984.63

Plate 81

- *Portrait Bust of Eliel Saarinen*
  (see plate 77)

  Sculpted by Eero Saarinen
  and cast probably in Yellow
  Springs, Ohio, 1930

  Cast bronze with oak base,
  14 x 6 ½ x 6 ¾ in.

  Collection of Robert
  Saarinen Swanson

Plate 82

Studio Alcove, view
from Studio

Plate 83

- *"Landing in New York"*
  (see plate 82)

  Painted by Zoltan Sepeshy,
  1935

  Oil on linen canvas, original
  frame; canvas, 25 x 30 in.;
  frame, 28 ½ x 33 ⅜ in.

  Collection of Robert
  Saarinen Swanson and
  Ronald Saarinen Swanson

Plate 84

- *"Head of a Dancing Girl"*

  Sculpted by Carl Milles and
  cast in Sweden, ca. 1917

  Cast bronze, patinated dark
  green, 18 ½ x 14 x 12 ½ in.

  Collection of Siri von Reis

Plate 82

Studio Alcove, view
from Studio

Plate 86

- *Vase*
  Designed by Vicke Lindstrand and produced by Orrefors Glasbruk, Sweden, ca. 1932
  Blown glass, 13 ⅞ x 8 ¼ in.
  Gift of J. Robert F. Swanson, 1981.18

Plate 87

- *Bar Buffet*
  Designed by J. Robert F. Swanson and possibly produced with the assistance of Tor Berglund, ca. 1932
  Wood and stainless steel, 40 ⅝₁₆ x 32 ⅝₁₆ x 18 ⅞ in.
  Gift of Robert Saarinen Swanson and Ronald Saarinen Swanson, 1979.3
- *"Gaiety" Cocktail Shaker*
  Designed by Howard Reichenbach, 1933, and produced by Chase Brass and Copper Company; patented and introduced 1934
  Spun and chrome-plated brass, 11 ⅛ x 3 ¹¹⁄₁₆ in.
  Gift of Jerome and Patricia Shaw, 1993.47
- *"Old Faithful" Seltzer Bottle* (not pictured)
  Produced in Czechoslovakia, after 1921
  Glass and metal, 13 ⅝ x 4 in.
  Gift of Ronald Saarinen Swanson, 1994.44

Plate 85

Studio and Studio Office, view from Studio Alcove

- *Hanging Lamps*
  Designed by Eliel Saarinen and produced by Edward F. Caldwell and Company, Inc., 1930
  Spun copper shades, lathe-turned brass hangers, all enameled; three lamps, each 56 ¼ x 18 in.
  1994.26.1.–.3
- *"Exhibition Rug"*
  Designed by Loja Saarinen and woven by Studio Loja Saarinen, 1932
  Linen warp, wool weft, wool pile; plain weave with *ryijy*-knotted pile, 324 x 141 in.; originally appx. 24 in. longer
  Gift of Pipsan Saarinen Swanson, 1980.9
- *Kingswood Auditorium Armchairs*
  Designed by Eero Saarinen with production attributed to Ypsilanti Reed Furniture Company, 1929–31
  Tubular chromed-steel, wood, and woven upholstery; seven chairs, each 31 x 21 ¼ x 26 ½ in.
  Collection of Cranbrook Schools (four chairs) and Cranbrook Academy of Art

Museum (three chairs), 1982.54 a, c, and d

- *"The Ballerina"*
  Drawn by Georgia Carroll, ca. 1930s (before April 1941)
  Graphite, charcoal, and conte crayon on cream paper; original frame, 21 ¹³⁄₁₆ x 18 ¼ in.; window, 15 x 11 ½ in.
  Collection of Robert Saarinen Swanson

Plate 88
Studio, Hanging Lamps by
Eliel Saarinen (see plate 85)

Plate 89

Studio

▪ *Credenza*

Designed by Eliel Saarinen
and made under the direction
of Tor Berglund, 1930

Wood with veneers; closed,
32 ¾ x 102 ⅞ x 36 in.;
extended, 32 ¾ x 102 ⅞ x
48 in.

1993.46

▪ *Wall Hanging: Ryijy Bridal Rug*

Woven in Finland, 1775

Linen warp, wool weft, wool
pile; plain weave with *ryijy*-
knotted pile front and back,
75 ½ x 66 ½ in.

Collection of Ronald
Saarinen Swanson

Plate 90

Studio

- *Flower Pot*

  Designed by Russel Wright
  and produced by
  Russel Wright Incorporated,
  ca. 1932

  Spun aluminum,
  5 ½ x 6 ¹⁵/₁₆ in.

  Collection of
  John C. Waddell

Plate 91

Studio

- *Set of Three Side Tables*

  Design attributed to Eero
  Saarinen and produced ca.
  1933

  Wood and aluminum; small,
  17 ¾ x 17 ¾ x 10 ¹/₁₆ in.;
  medium, 19 ¹¹/₁₆ x 20 ¹⁵/₁₆ x
  11 ⁵/₈ in.; large, 22 ¼ x 25 ¹³/₁₆
  x 13 ⁷/₁₆ in.

  Collection of Ronald
  Saarinen Swanson

Plate 92
Courtyard with *"Kivi's Muse"*
by Wäinö Aaltonen, view
from Studio (see plate 65)

Plate 93
Studio, view of Kingswood
Auditorium Armchairs by
Eero Saarinen (see plate 85)

Plate 94
Studio Office

- *Desk*

Designed by either Eliel Saarinen or Eero Saarinen and made under the direction of Tor Berglund, 1930

Wood with chromed-steel pulls, 30 1/16 x 63 9/16 x 35 15/16 in.

Gift of Ebba Brown, 1979.35

- *Reproduction Telephone Stand*

Original design attributed to Eliel Saarinen or J. Robert F. Swanson, ca. 1930s; reproduction made by Charles Phipps and Sons, Ltd., under the direction of Charles Phipps, 1993

Maple frame with maple veneers, 28 3/8 x 12 x 15 in.

Original in the collection of Ronald Saarinen Swanson

Reproduction in the collection of Cranbrook Academy of Art Museum, 1993.42

- *Side Chair*

Design attributed to Eero Saarinen, ca. 1929–31, with production possibly by Ypsilanti Reed Furniture Company, ca. 1929–31. Originally used in Living Room

Painted tubular steel with caning, 31 7/8 x 16 3/8 x 21 in.

1994.28

- *Adaptation Curtains*

Original design by Loja Saarinen and woven by Studio Loja Saarinen, ca. 1929–30; adaptations woven by Mary Anne Jordan, 1986–87, and hemmed by Anne Lindberg, 1988

Linen warp, linen weft; plain weave with continuous and discontinuous supplementary rayon wefts; two side panels, each 61 1/2 x 22 in.; valance, 10 x 97 1/2 in.

ZO 1988 10 a–c

- *Hanging Lamp*

Designed by Eliel Saarinen and produced by Edward F. Caldwell and Company, Inc., 1930

Spun copper shade, lathe-turned brass hangers, all enameled, 20 1/2 x 18 in.

1994.27

Plate 95
Studio and Studio Alcove

Plate 96

Studio Office

▪ *Desk Set*

Design attributed to Eliel
Saarinen and produced by
Svenskt Tenn, Sweden,
ca. 1935

Spun pewter vase and bowl,
fabricated pewter box with
cast handle; inkwell, 5 1/8 x
3 1/16 x 3 1/16 in.; vase, 3 13/16 x 4 x
4 in.; footed bowl, 2 3/16 x 2 9/16
x 2 9/16 in.

Gift of Robert Saarinen
Swanson and Ronald
Saarinen Swanson, 1993.1–.3

Plate 97

Adaptation Side Panel, detail
(see plate 94)

Plate 99
Studio Vestibule, view toward
Academy of Art Studio ·

Plate 100
Studio Vestibule, Leaded
Glass Window

Plate 98

Studio, view from
Studio Office

- *Curtain Side Panel and
  Valance Fragments*
  (not pictured)

  Designed by Loja Saarinen
  and woven by Studio Loja
  Saarinen, ca. 1929–30

  Linen warp, linen and wool
  weft; plain weave with
  supplementary wool wefts

  Gift of Anna Danielson,
  ZO 1982 9-10

- *Reproduction Curtains*

  Reproductions woven by
  Mary Anne Jordan,
  1986–87 and 1993, and
  hemmed by Anne Lindberg,

Rita Grendze, and Kate
Humphrey, 1988 and 1994

Linen warp, linen and wool
weft; plain weave with
supplementary wool wefts;
two north side-panels, each
75 ¾ x 31 in.; north valance,
12 x 278 in.; two south side-
panels, 61 x 28 ¾ in. and
61 x 26 ¾ in.; south valance,
12 x 126 in.
ZO 1988 11 a–c,
ZO 1988 12 a–b, 1994.29

Plate 101

Side Garden, Covered
Passage from Academy of
Art Studio to Saarinen House
Studio Entrance

Plate 102

Side Garden, Railing to
Saarinen House Studio
Entrance

Plate 103
Side Garden with dogwoods
in autumn color

Plate 104
Side Garden and Chimney,
view from Stairs to Triton Pool

Plate 107

Second Floor Hallway

▪ *Mouhijärvi Ryijy Rug*

Woven in Pirkanmaa,
Turku and Pori County,
Finland, 1788

Linen warp, wool weft,
wool pile; plain weave with
ryijy-knotted pile front and
back, 81 x 67 in.

Collection of Ronald
Saarinen Swanson

Plate 108

▪ Mouhijärvi *Ryijy* Rug, detail
(see plate 107)

Plate 109
Second Floor Hallway
Bathroom, view into Hallway

Plate 111

Second Floor Hallway

- *Adaptation Door Designs*
Original designs by Pipsan
Saarinen Swanson and

painted on shutters in the
Upper Dining Room at
Kingswood School for girls,
ca. 1931; adaptations painted
by Callie Johnson, 1993

Oil; nine designs, each
10 ³⁄₈ x 9 in.

Plate 112

Second Floor Hallway
Seating Alcove, view from
Son's Bedroom

Plate 110

Second Floor Hallway, view
from Seating Alcove

- *Bench*
Designed by Eliel Saarinen
and made by Tor Berglund,
1930
Painted wood, 30 ⁵⁄₁₆ x
103 ⁹⁄₁₆ x 22 ⅛ in.
1993.43

- *Table*
Designed by Eliel Saarinen
and made by Tor Berglund,
1930
Painted wood, 27 ⅞ x 30
x 30 in.
1993.45

- *Armchair*
Designed by Eliel Saarinen
and made by Tor Berglund,
1930
Painted wood, 30 ³⁄₁₆ x 23 ⅞
x 20 ¹³⁄₁₆ in.
1993.44

- *Adaptation Upholstery for
Bench and Armchair*
Original design by Loja
Saarinen and woven by
Studio Loja Saarinen,
ca. 1929–30; adaptation
designed by Paula Stebbins
Becker and woven by Craftex
Mills, Inc. of Penna., 1993
Rayon warp, cotton weft;
plain weave, bolt width
57 ³⁄₄ in.
Gift of Craftex Mills, Inc. of
Penna., 1994.12

- *Side Chair* (not pictured)
Design attributed to Eero
Saarinen, ca. 1929–31;
production possibly by
Ypsilanti Reed Furniture
Company, ca. 1929–31
Painted tubular steel with
caning, 31 ⅞ x 16 ³⁄₈ x 21 in.
1994.36

- *Beardslee #1024 Ceiling
Fixture* (in Seating Alcove)
Produced by Beardslee and
supplied by the Leonard
Electrical Company, 1930
Die-formed brass with
Flemish finish, 3 ½ x 6 ½ in.
1994.30.1

- *Reproduction Beardslee
Ceiling Fixture* (above
Stairway Landing)
Reproduction made by Brian
Meek, 1993
Spun, hammered, rolled, and
patinated brass, 3 ½ x 6 ½ in.
1994.31.1

- *Reproduction Alcove Rag Rug*
Original design attributed to
Maja Andersson Wirde or
Loja Saarinen and woven by
Studio Loja Saarinen, ca.
1930–31; reproduction

designed and woven by
Celeste Brush, 1993
Linen warp, weft of torn
cotton cloth strips; plain
weave with supplementary
weft inlays, 115 x 77 in.; with
fringe, 128 x 77 in.
1994.13

- *Adaptation Rag Rug for
Stairway Landing*
Adaptation designed and
woven by Celeste Brush,
1993
Linen warp, weft of torn
cotton cloth strips; plain
weave, 58 ¼ x 76 ¼ in.; with
fringe, 66 ³⁄₄ x 76 ¼ in.
1994.10

Plate 113

Second Floor Hallway
Seating Alcove

▪ *Reproduction Curtain for
Alcove*

Original design by Loja
Saarinen and woven by
Studio Loja Saarinen, ca.
1930; reproduction designed
by Paula Stebbins Becker and
woven by Paula Stebbins

Becker assisted by Laura
Sansone, 1992

Linen warp, lumpy tow linen
weft, and wool inlay; plain
weave with supplementary
weft inlay border; with fringe,
61 x 140 in.

1994.14

Plate 114

Reproduction Curtain, detail
(see plate 113)

Plate 115
Second Floor Hallway
Seating Alcove, view into
Master Bedroom

Plate 116

- *Portrait of Juliana Prange*
(see plate 115)

Sitter is Loja's great aunt.
Painted by M. Christian
Friedrich Prange, Germany,
1820

Oil on canvas, original frame;
canvas, 18 ⅞ x 15 ¾ in.;
frame, 23 ½ x 19 ¾ in.

Collection of B. Eric M.
Swanson

Plate 117

Banquette with Original
Upholstery and Lounge
Chair with Reproduction
Upholstery, detail
(see plate 118)

Plate 118

Master Bedroom

- *Table*
  Designed by Eero Saarinen and made by Tor Berglund, 1930
  Painted wood, 26 1/16 x 38 1/16 x 31 9/16 in.
  1984.20

- *Banquette Upholstery*
  Original design attributed to Loja Saarinen and woven by an unknown commercial manufacturer, ca. 1929–30
  Cotton warp, rayon or silk weft; Jacquard weave

- *Reproduction Lounge Chair for Master Bedroom*
  Original designed or supplied by J. Robert F. Swanson,

1930; reproduction designed and made by Charles Phipps and Sons, Ltd., under the direction of Charles Phipps, 1993
Solid maple frame and solid oak legs with vertical oak veneer and reproduction upholstery, 29 x 30 x 34 in.
1993.41

- *Reproduction Upholstery for Lounge Chair and Dressing Table Bench*
  Reproduction designed and woven by Sunbury Textile Mills, Inc., 1993
  Cotton warp, rayon weft; Jacquard weave, bolt width 58 in.
  Gift of Sunbury Textile Mills, Inc., 1994.15

- *Reproduction Rag Rug*
  Original design by Maja Andersson Wirde and woven by Studio Loja Saarinen, ca. 1930–31; reproduction designed and woven by Celeste Brush, 1992
  Linen warp, weft of torn cotton cloth strips; plain weave with supplementary weft inlays; 121 1/2 x 73 in.; with fringe, 136 1/2 x 73 in.
  1994.17

- *Portrait of Emilie Margarethe Struckmann Gesellius*
  Sitter is Loja's mother. Probably taken in Germany, nineteenth century
  Photograph, 9 1/16 x 9 in.
  Gift of Robert Saarinen Swanson and Ronald Saarinen Swanson, 1990.92

- *Portrait of Hermann Otto Gesellius*
  Sitter is Loja's father. Probably taken in Germany, nineteenth century
  Photograph, 9 1/16 x 9 in.
  Gift of Robert Saarinen Swanson and Ronald Saarinen Swanson, 1990.93

- *Portrait of Heinrich Friedrich Wilhelm Gesellius*
  Sitter is Loja's grandfather. Drawn in Germany, nineteenth century
  Graphite and white conte crayon on paper, 9 1/16 x 8 7/8 in.
  Gift of Robert Saarinen Swanson and Ronald Saarinen Swanson, 1990.94

Plate 120

- *Portrait of Heinrich Friedrich Wilhelm Gesellius*
(see plate 118)

Sitter is Loja's grandfather. Painted by Olli Ehrström in Finland, 1935, after a painting attributed to M. Christian Friedrich Prange painted in Germany, ca. 1830

Oil on canvas, original frame; canvas, 32 ⅛ x 28 ⅟₁₆ in.; frame, 35 ⅞ x 33 ¹³⁄₁₆ in.

Collection of Ronald Saarinen Swanson

Plate 121

- *Hanging Lamp* (see plate 118)

Designed by Eliel Saarinen and produced by Edward F. Caldwell and Company, Inc., 1930

Alabaster shade, lathe-turned and nickel-plated brass hangers, 34 ½ x 19 ½ in.

1994.32

Plate 119

Master Bedroom

- *Reproduction Curtains*

Original design attributed to Loja Saarinen, ca. 1930; reproductions designed and made by Christine Walsh and Laura Sansone, 1992, with fabric produced by Scalamandré, ca. 1992

Cotton voile with cotton piping; dressing table curtain, 94 x 188 in.; two south window curtains, 48 x 50 in.

1994.16.1–.3

- *Adaptation Skirt for Dressing Table*

Original design attributed to Loja Saarinen, ca. 1930; adaptation designed and made by Christine Walsh and Laura Sansone, 1992

Commercial cotton cloth, 123 x 27 ¼ in.

Plate 122

Master Bedroom

▪ *Dressing Table Mirror*

Designed by Eero Saarinen with production attributed to Edward F. Caldwell and Company, Inc., ca. 1930

Cast and silver-plated brass with nickel silver back; extended, 25 x 39 ¾ x 3 ¾ in.

ZO 1978 4

▪ *Dressing Table Lamps*

Designed by Eero Saarinen and produced by Edward F. Caldwell and Company, Inc., 1930

Cast brass bases and supports, fabricated nickel-silver shades, all silver-plated; two lamps, each 29 ⅟₁₆ x 7 ½ in.

ZO 1978 3

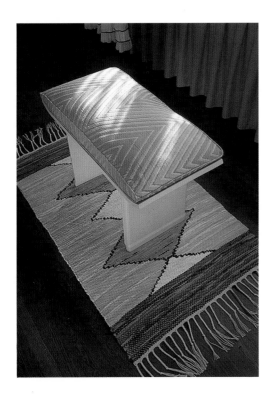

Plate 123

Master Bedroom

- *Dressing Table Bench*

Designed by Eero Saarinen and made by Tor Berglund, 1930

Painted wood, cushion with reproduction upholstery, 20 x 29 7/8 x 14 7/16 in.

1986.4

- *Reproduction Rag Rug for Dressing Table*

Original design attributed to Maja Andersson Wirde and woven by Studio Loja Saarinen, ca. 1930–31; reproduction designed by Celeste Brush, 1992, and woven by Celeste Brush, 1994

Linen warp, weft of torn cotton cloth strips; plain weave with supplementary weft inlays, 49 x 29 in.; with fringe, 62 x 29 in.

1994.18

Plate 124

Master Bedroom

- *Covered Box*

Repoussé and chasing attributed to Pipsan Saarinen Swanson on ready-made

covered box produced by S.H., Finland, 1921

813-gauge spun silver with repoussé and chasing, 1 x 3 3/8 in.

Collection of Sylvia Swanson-Gage

Plate 125

Master Bedroom

- *Dresser Set*

Design attributed to Eliel Saarinen and produced by International Silver Company, ca. 1934

Sterling silver with mirrored glass, wood, and bristles; hand mirror, 11 3/8 x 5 1/16 x 9/16 in.; hair brush, 8 1/4 x 3 1/4 x 1 5/16 in.; comb, 7 11/16 x 1 7/8 x 3/16 in.; clothes brush, 7 x 2 1/8 x 1 1/2 in.; shoe horn, 8 3/8 x 1 9/16 x 7/16 in.

Collection of Karen Swanson Austin

- *Hairbrush*

Produced in the United States, ca. 1934

Silver, paint, wood, and bristles, 7 15/16 x 2 7/16 x 1 1/4 in.

Collection of Robert Saarinen Swanson

Plate 129

Master Bathroom

- *Reproduction Curtains for Windows*

  Original design attributed to Loja Saarinen, ca. 1930; reproductions designed and made by Christine Walsh and Laura Sansone, 1992, with fabric produced by Scalamandré, ca. 1992

  Cotton voile with cotton piping; four curtains, each 37 ⅛ x 34 ⅜ in.

  1994.20.1–.4

- *Adaptation Curtains for Shower and Water Closet*

  Original designs made ca. 1930; adaptations designed and made by Kristen Dettoni, 1992

  Commercial cotton cloth; shower, 82 x 63 ¾ in.; water closet, 85 x 63 ¾ in.

Plate 130

Master Bathroom, view out the window toward Academy of Art Dormitory in spring with dogwood in bloom

Plate 128

Master Bathroom, view from Master Bedroom

- *Bath Mat* (hanging)

  Design attributed to Loja Saarinen, ca. 1929–30

  Tufted rayon pile with canvas backing, 48 ½ x 24 in.

  Gift in part of Ronald Saarinen Swanson, ZO 1983 120

- *Adaptation Bath Mat* (on floor)

  Adaptation made by Kay Dawson, 1983

  Linen warp, cotton weft, rayon pile; plain weave with *ryijy*-knotted pile, 44 ¾ x 24 in.

  ZO 1983 124

Plate 132
Side Garden, Gate to Rear
Garden, detail

Plate 131
Side Garden, view of Gate to
Rear Garden with
Cranbrook Academy of Art
Museum in the distance

Plate 133
Courtyard in summer

Plate 134
Courtyard in autumn with
winged euonymus

Plate 135
Courtyard in spring with
tulips in bloom

Plate 136
Courtyard in winter

Plate 137

Courtyard, view from Porch

- *Pair of Garden Urns*

  Design attributed to Mary
  Chase Perry Stratton and
  possibly thrown by Joseph
  Heerick or Julius Albus for
  Pewabic Pottery under the
  direction of Mary Chase
  Perry Stratton, ca. 1915–25

  Thrown ceramic with molded,
  applied, and scraped patterns, and glazed with
  Pewabic "K4" glaze,
  each 31 1/2 x 19 1/4 in.

  1931.42 a–b

- *Lounge Chairs* (not pictured)

  Design attributed to Eero
  Saarinen, ca. 1929–31;
  production possibly by
  Ypsilanti Reed Furniture
  Company, ca. 1929–31

  Painted tubular steel with
  caning; two chairs,
  each 27 3/8 x 21 1/8 x 27 1/4 in.

  1994.41–.42

- *Side Chairs* (not pictured)

  Design attributed to Eero
  Saarinen, ca. 1929–31;
  production possibly by
  Ypsilanti Reed Furniture
  Company, ca. 1929–31

  Painted tubular steel with
  caning; four chairs,
  each 31 7/8 x 16 3/8 x 21 in.

  1994.37–.40

Plate 138

Courtyard in winter

Plate 139

Courtyard in early autumn
with anemones in bloom and
"Kivi's Muse" by Wäinö
Aaltonen, view from Porch
(see plate 65)

Plate 140
Porch, Door to Kitchen

Plate 141

Porch

- *"Wrestlers" Tile*
  (see plate 140)

  Designed by Eero Saarinen and produced by Pewabic Pottery under the direction of Mary Chase Perry Stratton, ca. 1928

  Ceramic, set in wall,
  12 ⅞ x 8 ½ in.

Plate 142

Porch

- *"Tragedy" Tile*

  Produced at Pewabic Pottery under the direction of Mary Chase Perry Stratton, ca. 1929–30

  Glazed ceramic, set in wall,
  6 ⅜ x 6 ¼ in.

Plate 143

Porch

- *"Comedy" Tile*

  Possibly designed by Eero Saarinen and produced at Pewabic Pottery under the direction of Mary Chase Perry Stratton, ca. 1929–30

  Glazed ceramic, set in wall,
  6 ⅜ x 6 ½ in.

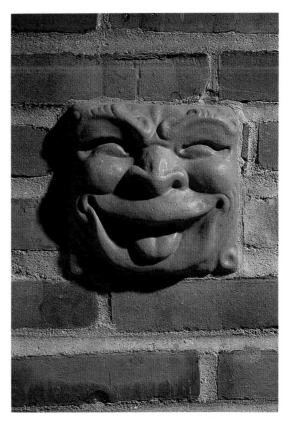

Plate 144
Saarinen House (left) and
Milles House in early autumn,
view from across Triton Pool

Plate 145
Saarinen House in spring,
view from Triton Pool

Plate 146
Triton Pool in late spring
with chestnut tree in bloom,
view from Courtyard

Plate 147

Courtyard in early autumn,
view from Maid's Bedroom
Window

SAARINEN HOUSE GARDEN

Diana Balmori

THE ART OF LANDSCAPE AT CRANBROOK

In spirit Hvitträsk hovers behind the Saarinens' garden at Cranbrook. Located on the shore of Lake Vitträsk, west of Helsinki, Finland, Hvitträsk was the studio and personal home of the trio of architects Herman Gesellius, Armas Lindgren, and Eliel Saarinen. Loja Gesellius took up residence with her brother in 1903, and married Eliel in 1904. Lindgren moved out in 1905, and Gesellius's part in the collaboration ended in 1907. Eliel then took over the whole studio, although the north wing of Hvitträsk remained Gesellius's home until his death. As both studio and home, Hvitträsk embodied the widely held belief among artists at the turn of the century that work, art, and life should be an indivisible whole. Built and ready for occupancy in 1904, it stood against the separation of work and life that industrialization was bringing about at the time. These ideas, expressed most clearly by the Arts and Crafts movement in its European versions, would manifest themselves in the United States as well, particularly at Cranbrook Academy of Art. There, Eliel Saarinen served as both architect from 1925 to 1950 and president from 1932 to 1946. The resonances between Hvitträsk and Cranbrook throw light on the Saarinens' work at Cranbrook.

The use of vines to wrap both houses comes first to mind. At Hvitträsk, vines completely covered the lower stone walls of the house and created the impression that it was entirely a wooden building (fig. 38). At Saarinen House at Cranbrook, as well as in Eliel's drawings of the other Cranbrook buildings he designed, vines are ubiquitous and always important. Vines might seem a small detail with which to start the story of this garden, but they weave together the two studio homes and reveal a principle of the Arts and Crafts movement that informs the design of both places. This principle, lost with the rise of the International Style, sought to join architecture and landscape, and explored ways of crossing the conceptual and philosophical lines that separate the two. The use of vines as green screens spreading over building walls is a device to achieve such a passage between the natural and built environments.

The Picturesque movement at the beginning of the eighteenth century first confronted this divide, and its earliest designers proposed solutions of connec-

tion and continuity.[1] One solution carried out in the period from 1710 to 1750 consisted of the use of hermitages, grottos, and ruins—constructions buried in the earth, half caves, crumbling walls overtaken by growing plants, and other liminal structures that mediated between architecture and landscape. By the 1750s, however, discrete rules for each of the two arts had developed, and the degree to which intermediate pieces could effectively respond to either architecture or landscape began to be ques-

Figure 39
Cranbrook Academy of Art,
aerial view of Academy Way
(left) and the Art Museum
(right). Photographed
ca. 1942

tioned. Such pieces began to be viewed simply as clutter in the landscape. In the nineteenth century, conceptual efforts within the Arts and Crafts movement once again attempted to address the division between architecture and landscape. Such efforts are exemplified in Cranbrook's landscape, both in the immediate vicinity of buildings, as in the Saarinen House garden, installed in 1930, and in the larger-scale landscape of roads, woods, and topography, developed from 1905 to 1923. In the Saarinens' garden, the intermediate space of the courtyard serves as a transition between building and landscape and addresses connections between interior and exterior. In the courtyard, for example, vines hung as outdoor draperies. Vistas and exterior, large-scale repetitions of interior details were also attempts at such connections. This interplay between architecture and landscape is precisely what is most valuable in the small garden of Saarinen House. The details of the connection between interior and exterior, between architecture and landscape, are the focus of this essay. When the Saarinens and American landscape architect C. Deforest Platt were at work on the garden, both architecture and landscape design in America and Europe were in a period of dramatic change. For this reason, it will be useful to outline here the artistic concepts that governed the overall design of Cranbrook and to chart their trajectories of development and change.

George Booth, a Detroit newspaper publisher and a founder of the Detroit Society of Arts and Crafts in 1906, formally founded Cranbrook Academy of Art in 1927 as a vehicle of expression for the Arts and Crafts movement (fig. 39). It was for the creation of the art academy that Eliel Saarinen finally stayed in the United States. In his first description of the academy, George Booth offered its theoretical and pedagogical principles: the integration of the various arts and an emphasis on self-education through art; the academy as a teaching place where artists do not formally teach but rather serve as guides and examples as they go about their art.[2] These ideas were given concrete form in Eliel Saarinen's first design for the academy, from which Loja Saarinen sculpted a clay model. Booth wrote a curriculum for the academy, which included landscape among its arts and horticulture among its crafts. In Eliel's plan and Loja's model, the School of Landscape is a large building centrally located along one of the main axes; included are large greenhouses for the study of horticulture (see Wittkopp, fig. 3).

Booth destroyed the model a few years after it was built, fearing it was evidence of Cranbrook's shortcomings, a failure to fulfill its vision. Certainly that vision had changed: landscape had disappeared from the curriculum by the 1930s, and the buildings for landscape and horticulture were never built. But there was more behind these changes than the curtailment of a single institution's founding vision. The secondary role accorded to the profession of landscape as Cranbrook grew and matured represented major shifts taking place among the arts in America and Europe as the modern movement, which began with the Arts and Crafts concepts, moved gradually toward what we know as the International Style.

Cranbrook's artistic continuity has been important enough to qualify it as one of the most successful Arts and Crafts schools. The history of Cranbrook has been gathered in a 1983 volume entitled *Design in America: The Cranbrook Vision, 1925–1950,* which covers the evolution of the different arts at Cranbrook.[3] This book, however, does not deal with landscape. And yet Cranbrook's landscape was an intrinsic part of its image and philosophy, and remained so in spite of the modifications in program and vision implemented by Booth and the designers he hired in its later years.

Elsewhere I have outlined the development of Cranbrook's landscape, from Booth's first vision of the area as a farm, to that of a great estate, to that of a campus whose landscape of high artistic quality was a place for the use and enjoyment of an artistic community.[4] The landscape designers H. W. Corfield and O. C. Simonds shaped the initial, overall landscape. (Corfield, an English landscaper, had planned the gardens of Booth's house. Simonds established the concept of large forests of single species.) At various times in the later life of the institution, the Olmsted Brothers' firm, Platt, A. E. Eichstaedt, and Loja Saarinen all played roles in Cranbrook's gradually diminishing landscape program. The story of Cranbrook, therefore, serves to document the changed status of landscape art as the International Style gained ascendancy. This development in the visual arts affected the design of the Saarinens' garden, as the enclosed courtyard that prevailed in the design of the boys' school, an earlier building, gradually gave way to the partially enclosed platform or terrace. The best expressions of the later style at Cranbrook are the peristyle of the Academy of Art Museum, the terraces around the Orpheus Fountain, and the terraces along the Triton Pool, which became the main view from the garden of Saarinen House (fig. 40). Fortunately for Cranbrook, some of the major decisions made regarding landscape shaped the sites before most of the buildings were constructed; the structures built subsequent to these decisions, therefore, have an integrity of design that distinguishes them from most educational institutions built in America after Cranbrook.

Saarinen House was designed and built between 1928 and 1930. The Saarinens moved into their new home in September of 1930, and they continued to

work on it for the next few years. The Booth residence, known as Cranbrook House (Albert Kahn, designer, 1907–08, 1918–20), the Greek Theater (Marcus Burrowes, 1915), Brookside School (George G. Booth, 1918, and Henry S. Booth, 1928–29), Christ Church Cranbrook (Bertram Grosvenor Goodhue Associates, 1924–28), Cranbrook School for boys (primarily Eliel Saarinen, 1925–28), and the site's overall landscaping and road construction preceded Saarinen House. Milles House on Academy Way (Eliel Saarinen, 1928–30) was contemporaneous with it. Kingswood School for girls (1929–31), the Institute of Science (1935–38), and the Academy of Art (1927–38) and Museum and Library (1938–42) were all designed primarily by Eliel Saarinen and constructed after Saarinen House.

As the Saarinen residence was designed and built immediately after the boys' school, the two belong to the same era and style of Saarinen building. The landscape program for the residence, however, was smaller than that accorded to earlier Cranbrook projects. Booth is known to have had a great interest in landscape, and until about 1921 to 1923, he gave

Corfield and Simonds a large scope in the complexity and scale of, and budget for, their designs. By the time Saarinen House was being planned, both Corfield and Simonds were gone (the latter had finished his work at Cranbrook by 1926). It was Platt, as a consultant on a monthly salary, who planted

Figure 40
Cranbrook Academy of Art, Triton Pool with *Europa and the Bull.* Photographed ca. late 1930s

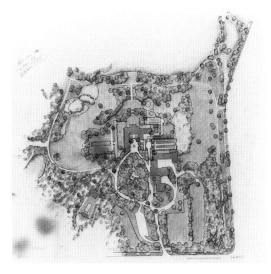

Figure 41

Cranbrook House, Plan of
the Terraces and Gardens.
Drawing ca. 1960s.
Collection Cranbrook
Archives, AD.04.56

Figure 42

Saarinen House and Garden
and the Triton Pool, Sectional
Drawing. Drawing by Patricia
Crow, 1994

Cranbrook's courtyards of this period. Although we
have no plan drawn by Platt for the garden of
Saarinen House itself, we do know that it shared the
same plant palette and a similar disposition of plants
with these other gardens. Platt and his work at
Cranbrook will be discussed in greater detail later in
this essay.

SAARINEN HOUSE GARDEN

In a close examination of the Saarinen House garden there is the danger of getting lost in the
multitude of its details. This discussion will attempt
both to distinguish and to synthesize the garden's
most important characteristics. There are two formal elements in the garden's design that express two
distinct but harmonizing principles of artistic order-
ing. The first and more pronounced element is the
garden's section, which Eliel Saarinen designed. The
second presides quietly as a network of visual and
associative correspondences between formal features of the garden and rooms of the house adjoining
the garden. The subtle texture of this element of the
design was most probably the work of Loja Saarinen.

The design of the cross-section in contemporary
landscape is perhaps the most neglected aspect of
landscape work, due in part to the International
Style's understanding of architecture as an object
posed on a site but not interacting with it. The section was considerably more important in

Renaissance and Picturesque landscapes from the
fifteenth through the eighteenth centuries, and it is
the place at which to start a detailed analysis of the
Saarinens' garden.

To understand the originality of the Saarinen section, we might first turn briefly to the Cranbrook
House garden, which was built most likely between
1912 and 1916. Comparison of the Booth and
Saarinen gardens reveals two different phases in the
Arts and Crafts movement and two different solutions to the section: in the Booth garden we find a
section directly based on historical precedent; in the
Saarinen case, we see a fresh approach to terracing
(figs. 41, 42).

The section and plan of the Booth garden follow the
reinterpretation and Americanization of the tradition of the Italian hill gardens of the late
Renaissance. The work of Charles Platt, dissemi-
nated through the articles and editorials of Herbert
Croly in *The Architectural Record,* and of Edith
Wharton, first popularized in a series of *House
Beautiful* articles and published in book form, the
influential *Italian Villas and Their Gardens* of 1905,
established this fashion. The Booth garden fits solidly
into this popular tradition; the Saarinen House garden, in contrast, lays claim to an originality of design
and philosophy.

The Booth house is sited on a hill; its Italianate gardens cascade down the hill in the form of terraces,
which were designed as sets of rooms in a classical
layout. Walls and hedges lend their crisp edges to
each level. Cranbrook House is a full mansion with a
garden of estate proportions. Saarinen House, on
the other hand, is a row house set between a neighboring house and studios, its garden that of a
middle-class residence. The different strategies of
terracing, however, remain indicative of the two

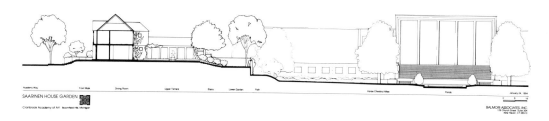

gardens' essential differences. The Booth garden is a historical exercise derived from East Coast Italianate gardens; each stands on its own, each has a discrete scheme, style, and character of planting following established formulas and menus. The garden of Saarinen House, on the other hand, employs the Arts and Crafts dictum of transition; the movement from courtyard to garden is a dynamic continuum and both elements lead the visitor into a larger view of a very well designed and contained space.

The Section

In figure 42 we see that the section is the principal feature of the Saarinen House garden. The Saarinen residence exploits the contours of its site; the terracing of the garden is dynamic. The visitor moves from the upper courtyard down a set of central steps to the lower garden of grass, flowers, and trees. In this movement through the garden, the long, rich vistas of its landscape reveal themselves in layers: the gaze moves across the courtyard, the steps, the lower level, over the wall to the formal, stepped fountain of the main academy space and to the woods beyond.

The photographs of the garden during the Saarinens' era reveal its dynamic nature by documenting the vital role it played in the life of the household (figs. 43–45). During warm weather, the daily life of the house, its rituals and gatherings, all were staged on and against the backdrop of the garden's two tiers. The upper tier is a paved terrace off

the dining room, and it steps down six feet—about the height of a person—to the lower tier, the garden proper, planted with grass, three elm trees, and roses against the garden wall. Spreading out from the stairs, the lower garden creates a natural balcony, where, as the photographs show, people tended to congregate. The movement from the edge of the upper terrace down the stairs to the lower garden forms a kind of theater of expectation and convergence, which makes each part of the garden an appealing place to stand, gather, and socialize. The steps in the center did not simply connect the two tiers but formed a significant part of the backdrop and stage for the Saarinens' social gatherings. It is difficult today, without using the archival photographs, to evoke from views of the empty garden how each element of it participated in shaping the character of those gatherings; together they formed a space resembling a narrow and crowded sidewalk—the kind of space, as William Whyte has shown in his studies of use of space in New York City, where people like to congregate.[5]

To preserve the garden's design, nothing should attenuate the experience of moving between the two levels of courtyard and garden, nothing should obstruct the views that open out from these two tiers. Tall or massive trees below the low garden wall would interrupt the views of the cascading tiers of the linear fountain with the Milles sculptures— *Europa and the Bull,* installed in 1935, and the figures of the Triton Pool, installed in 1938—of the horse chestnut alley (fig. 46) and, in winter, when the chestnuts have shed their leaves, of the pine forest

Figure 43

Saarinen House, Courtyard, with (left to right) Pipsan Saarinen Swanson, Carolyn Booth (wife of Henry Booth), J. Robert F. Swanson, and Loja Saarinen. May 20, 1947

Figure 44

Saarinen House, Courtyard, Garden Stairs, during a party for students. May 20, 1947

Figure 45

Saarinen House, Lower Garden overlooking the Triton Pool, during a party for students. May 1936

Figure 46

Cranbrook Academy of Art, Triton Pool and Chestnut Alley. Photographed August 1993

beyond, and would betray the intention of the garden's design. The three elms that once grew in the lower level of the garden conformed with the design since they were willowy and their high-limbed trunks and light canopies did not obstruct the view.

The Plan: Interplay of Interior and Exterior

The second important feature of the Saarinen garden is its careful interplay with the house's interior.

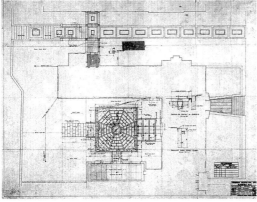

Figure 47

Saarinen House, Courtyard, Paving Plan. Drawing by Fred C. Thompson, April 16, 1930. Collection Cranbrook Archives AD.11.599

Figure 48

Stockholm Cemetery by Gunnar Asplund, pavers in grass. Photographed ca. 1992

This articulation of formal and associative connections between elements of the garden and the interior of the house was most probably the work of Loja Saarinen. For, though much documentation of her work is lacking, the impress of her hand is evident in both elements of the interior—in the design of most of the curtains, rugs, and a wall hanging—and elements in the landscape.

The visitor approaches the house along steps that gradually telescope toward the front door. The front gardens between the house and the street are at the level of the top step. A brick retaining wall encloses the garden's small lawn. Upon entering the building, one has only a veiled view of the rear garden from the entrance hall. Direct encounter of it is withheld until one moves into the dining room. It is the dining room that opens into intimate relation with the garden. One can enter the garden from the studio but this room does not have the same kind of privileged relation to the garden.

The square plan of the dining room is notched slightly by corner cupboards, and this modifies the room's shape to an octagon (see Wittkopp, fig. 6). The square rug in the room repeats this theme, for it bears an octagonal pattern. The base of the dining table is also octagonal. Immediately beyond the two bifold glass doors, which open to the garden in front of the table, a square, paved terrace with grassed joints mirrors the dimensions of the dining room and serves as an entrance to the larger area of the upper courtyard. The upper courtyard is a paved octagon with grassed joints, translating the shape of the dining room into the larger scale appropriate to an exterior, unroofed space. In the original plan, this octagon within a square also has its corners notched (fig. 47). The pavers of the octagon have grassed

joints, while the corner triangles outside the octagon have sand joints. The effect is not unlike that of a woven tapestry, and not unlike the paving at Stockholm Cemetery by Gunnar Asplund (fig. 48), the work often cited as inspiration for the Cranbrook Academy of Art Museum peristyle. Another delicate detail participates in weaving this pattern of correspondences between interior and exterior: a tapestry bearing the image of a tree, purchased by the Saarinens from Finnish weaver Greta Skogster between 1935 and 1939, hangs on the wall opposite the glass garden doors as if reflecting one of the elms in the lower garden.

In the upper courtyard, vines, ceramics and sculpture articulate the connections between the house and the garden. All vertical planes are covered with English or Boston ivy; on the north side of the courtyard, a wisteria runs along the eave of the summer porch, as if to ensure that all enclosed sides are clothed in leaves. Two niches in the walls of the courtyard occasionally held ceramic vases. Immediately outside the dining room stood turquoise urns made by Pewabic Pottery. Pottery in general was a very important part of the Arts and Crafts aesthetic. In the Detroit area, the Pewabic Pottery, under the direction of Mary Chase Perry Stratton, played a central role in inspiring the use of ceramics in both indoor and outdoor spaces. The two urns, recently returned to the Saarinen House garden, can be seen in photos of the actors' court in the Greek Theater circa 1925 and in photos of the Saarinen House garden dating from 1930. There was also sculpture in the center of the upper courtyard: *Kivi's Muse,* by Finnish sculptor Wäinö Aaltonen, cast in bronze and purchased by George Booth through Loja Saarinen in 1930 for Cranbrook. In Finland it originally formed part of a much larger sculptural grouping in which the muse is touching the head of Finnish writer Aleksis Kivi with her hand.

The whole panoply of spatial forms, of objects—tapestry, carpet, furniture, plantings, pavements, vine-covered walls, sculpture, and ceramics—conspired to create the transitions between the house and garden. This remarkable union of media to suggest a fluid harmony between spaces that traditionally were clearly distinguished was itself a product of collaboration between Loja and Eliel Saarinen. It also represents the best of Arts and Crafts ideas at work: the dissolution and reinterpretation of the assumed boundary between artifice and nature, building and landscape.

We know of Loja's work as the head of the academy's Department of Weaving and Textile Design and of Studio Loja Saarinen from official papers and from correspondence. Among the letters is the exchange between Loja and Frank Lloyd Wright about the weaving of textiles for the Kaufmann office in Pittsburgh. It is only in a document concerning Loja's dismissal from her position as head of Cranbrook's weaving studio, however, that we find a verification of her work in the early 1940s in landscape and interiors: "As you know, besides being the head of the weaving department, I have also supervised the interior decoration at the Academy and for the last two years I have, with your consent, planned the planting around the Museum building."[6] There is also an extant drawing of Loja's that introduces a hedge of junipers in the academy's main axis along the plinth by the main steps. Eliel's drawings for Cranbrook do show the use of vines, as they did in Hvitträsk, but do not show hedges.[7]

From these documents it is difficult to establish the extent of Loja's contributions to the design of the Saarinens' residence and garden, or to other aspects of Cranbrook as a whole. To do so requires a shift in the type of sources one must employ. Supporting archival materials are missing when the work of women is not publicly acknowledged by a title, position, or salary. The documents that are generated are often discarded as unimportant—merely the product of leisure. Thus women's contributions in many fields remain undiscerned or, if perceived, undervalued for lack of insight. Many times we discover evidence of a woman's contribution in the asides, the casual mentions of her activity in documents pertaining to other matters. Such is the case with Loja Saarinen and the landscape at Cranbrook.

When the written records of women's work are meager, one also turns to the evidence of oral histories. A few of Loja's contemporaries can recall her activity at Cranbrook. Dominick Vettraino, the son of Cranbrook's head gardener, Mike Vettraino, and eventually the head gardener himself for many years, remembers going with his father every fall to meet with Loja and get her patterned, color drawings of planting beds with a list of the plants she needed to have grown for the spring.[8] Marianne Strengell, Loja's successor in the weaving department, remembers her interest in gardening at Hvitträsk and Cranbrook.[9] Anna Danielson, the

Figure 49
Saarinen House, with Eliel
Saarinen in front of Dorothy
Perkins climbing roses.
ca. 1943

Figure 50
Cranbrook Academy of Art,
Boys' School Headmaster's
Residence, Garden Plan,
Designed by C. Deforest
Platt. Drawing by D. K. H.,
November 18, 1929.
Collection Cranbrook
Archives, AD.11.3

Saarinens' housekeeper as well as a weaver in
Studio Loja Saarinen, recalls Loja's role in the garden as that of a "strong person" who "kept things
rolling," and states that as for the interiors, "Loja held
the strings in the house."[10] As sources of information,
a couple of Loja's sketches of the plantings in the
main courtyard of the academy, a typed note on a list
of furnishings she was leaving at her Cranbrook
house that mentions she will pick up her perennials
on October 1,[11] and the documents regarding Loja's
work as a landscape designer are exhausted. A
search for her drawings for patterned plantings—
Dominick Vettraino recalls that they were
"like her weavings"—has proved unsuccess-
ful. The Cranbrook greenhouse has kept no
records, and the commercial nursery that
grew plants for Cranbrook went out of business in 1985 and discarded all of its
records.[12]

Despite the fact that the only extant documentation for the house's courtyard and
garden is a plan in Eliel's hand and that the
rug with the octagonal pattern was
designed by Eliel for a museum exhibition
and used in the dining room, the quiet mir-
roring between the living and the tapestried
trees, the sculpture and its placement in the

center of the octagon, the formal echo in the garden
of interior elements—the carpet and the curtains—
and the crisp borders of the barberry hedges all
bear witness to Loja's artistic influence in and contribution to the garden's design.

The Plantings

Of all the garden's plantings, the vines are the most
important and most clearly situate the garden within
the Arts and Crafts era. Several varieties are found
throughout the grounds: English and Boston ivy
(*Hedera helix* and *Parthenocissus tricuspidata*) on the
front of the house and on the courtyard walls; roses
used as vines grow on the front and back garden
walls; wisteria and clematis are also present. The use
of vines for their draping and softening effect on
walls is a major aspect of Arts and Crafts design. At
Saarinen House, roses rarely appear in shrub form
but as ramblers or climbers (fig. 49). The Dorothy
Perkins rambling rose in the front of the house is typical of their use: it is tied to a continuous wire
running along the front of the street wall and provides a crisp line of greenery and flowers along the
street. This feature is repeated in Milles House next
door and in the other faculty houses across the
street.

The overall plant layout and species selection can be
attributed to C. Deforest Platt, a landscape archi-

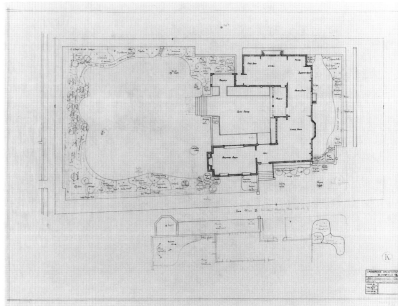

tect about whom we know little. In 1924 he graduated from Harvard, where he won a class prize for being one of the two best students, and was consequently sent to Italy. He lived in Detroit and his only other known work is his restoration of Fort Necessity, a battle site where Washington fought.[13] At Cranbrook he was on a retainer of $250 a month (approximately $2,000 in 1990 dollars). He was responsible for the planting of the whole boys' school site and of the grounds of the residences along Academy Way. In the archives there is an extant plan of Saarinen House that bears his office seal, but it does not include any of his plantings. The plan for the boys' school headmaster's residence, the building immediately across the street from the Saarinen residence, also bears his seal and does include the plantings. Judging from the way the plants have been organized in the Saarinen House garden, and from the planting list for the headmaster's residence, it is likely that Platt was responsible for Saarinen House garden's general planting, which was probably varied and enriched by Eliel and Loja Saarinen. For instance, the barberry hedges that border the planting areas and give structure to the garden are not a device Platt used elsewhere at Cranbrook, nor are formal, clipped hedges a part of his vocabulary on the campus. The marked presence of such an architectonic element as a barberry hedge in the Saarinen House garden, therefore, convinces us of Eliel and Loja Saarinen's intervention in the garden's design.

Platt's plant list for the headmaster's residence employs a spatial arrangement and plant palette similar to those of the Saarinen garden. The parallels are obtained in the overall use of common plants, such as *Viburnum, Spiraea, Philadelphus, Euonymus, Lonicera, Cornus,* and *Syringa*; in the use of rambling and weeping forms of shrubs, such as *Rosa, Forsythia,* and *Weigela*; and the frequent use of vines, such as wisteria and clematis.

A striking parallel in the gardens of the two residences lies in the varieties of *Lonicera* used: *Lonicera tatarica* 'Rosea,' *Lonicera maacki, Lonicera morrowii, Lonicera kerakowi,* and *Lonicera fragrantissima.* On

the other hand, a noticeable difference between the two plantings is the complete absence of ivies in the headmaster's residence. The ivies of the Saarinen residence appear to indicate the Saarinens' choice and return us to their villa in Finland, Hvitträsk. The use of ivies on walls, the use of clipped barberry hedges (*Berberis thunbergii*) to define the space in the upper courtyard, and the use of garden steps are not evident in any of the other plantings by Platt. Ivies are present on the walls of the boys' school, but they are found specifically on Eliel's elevation drawings, again pointing to a Saarinen decision.

A comparison of the plans for the Saarinen residence and the headmaster's residence (fig. 50) shows that the front gardens of both have lawn panels with compact shrubs placed in each of their corners, and Dorothy Perkins rambling roses running along the retaining walls of both gardens, so that the rose foliage and flowers cover a portion of the walls. The two gardens have, as do those of the other residences at Cranbrook, many overlapping plant species, and the list represents an Arts and Crafts philosophy of planting. Landscape design from 1890 through 1930, as influenced by the Arts and Crafts movement, favored vernacular and regional plantings. The plants, often considered common weeds, were ordinary, native varieties, vigorous and hearty in their indigenous growing conditions. Such landscaping shunned the imported, exotic, rare, foreign, or delicate plant.

In addition, Arts and Crafts ideas opposed the "bedding out" practice introduced in Victorian gardens in England, in which the flowering annuals were pulled out as soon as their flowers had faded to be replaced with newly flowering plants. This style of planting relied on the growing of homogeneous flowering annuals in massive quantities in large, commercial greenhouses. Instead, Arts and Crafts practitioners suggested planting and growing perennials on site. The opposition to the bedding out of homogeneous annuals was not only an aesthetic difference, it was also a protest against industrialization and its treatment of living things. It was the relationship of landscape design with nature, the fact that as an art it dealt with living things, that ultimately prevented it from adopting the terms of industrialization. As the other arts embraced the industrial age and marched into the period of the International Style, landscape remained ambivalent, conceptually tied to a crafts approach; it thereby held back as a discipline and fell away from the forces affecting the other visual arts. In turn, the retention of craft labor signaled the demise of landscape design. When labor costs rose dramatically after the Depression, only one type of landscape, aside from agriculture, made the shift into the industrial era: the landscape of the lawn, which became the ubiquitous landscape of the International Style.

The Lawn

The garden of Saarinen House represented a transition in American landscape design. A good percentage of it was taken up by grass and lawn, and it made the shift into the modern era in that it was installed and cared for using modern machines. Dominick Vettraino noted that throughout his lifetime, sod was brought from sod farms and installed in the Saarinen House garden and throughout the grounds at Cranbrook as a whole.

Cranbrook lawns were seeded and existing sodded lawns were reseeded, however, with a more diverse mix of seeds, which reflected older practices that produced less homogeneous lawns. Until the end of World War II, the grass used for lawns contained a percentage of either white or red clover, and sometimes both. Through interviews with Mr. Vettraino, it was possible to recover the grass mix used at Cranbrook when he and, before him, his father were head gardeners. The mix was half Kentucky bluegrass, half perennial rye, with white clover and red clover mixed in. Bent grass was also used when sod was brought in from the outside, usually purchased from the Godwin Sod Farm in nearby South Lyon.

The Garden Over Time: After World War II

Landscape lives and dies. In this small garden major changes have occurred over time. Some came

Figure 51

Saarinen House, Courtyard, with Eliel Saarinen in front of hollyhocks. ca. 1948

Figure 52

Saarinen House, Lower Garden, with Loja Saarinen and George Booth in front of *Spiraea* bushes. May 1936

about through the vicissitudes in the lives of those living in the house and garden, some by the plants' process of growth, maturity, decay, and death. The appearance of flowering perennials in the garden after 1939, for example, reflects an alteration in the Saarinens' lifestyle when the Second World War broke out. Previously the Saarinens had spent the summer months at Hvitträsk. But when World War II kept them at Cranbrook for the summers, Loja began planting flowering perennials for their enjoyment (fig. 51). Photographs and home movies of the

1940s show a variety of flowering perennials in the garden: hollyhocks and anemones around the planted edges of the upper terrace, campanulas and iris against the garden wall, and low flowering aubrieta around the sculpture in the center of the upper courtyard.

If a change in the life of the garden's owners led to a new profusion of flowers in the summer garden, Platt's choice of native and naturalized plants resulted in a succession of changes in the life of the garden. By the time of the garden's restoration, two of the shrubs used sparsely in the original planting,

Lonicera morrowii and *Lonicera tatarica*, had spread thickly over the side and main garden. The small beech by the porch off the upper courtyard had grown overly large, and its thick shade prevented the survival of the *Spiraea* shrubs (fig. 52).

A garden has been defined as nature in a state of arrested development. The *Lonicera* invasion can be interpreted as failure to maintain this arrested state. But it can also be seen as a test of survivability, and *Lonicera,* in its easy spread, displays the characteristics of a weed or an indigenous plant. In a well-maintained garden, this spread can be controlled and put to good use, allowing such plants to fill in where other plants have failed.

The biggest change in any garden is in its trees, and the Saarinen House garden is no exception. The loss of elms to Dutch elm disease in the early 1970s affected the Saarinen House garden dramatically: the house lost the graceful canopy extending the whole length of the street in front; in the back garden, the three elms planted in the lower tier, which lent a sense of privacy and separateness to the garden (fig. 53), were also lost. The rotting remnants of the lost elms' roots were still clearly visible in depressions in the back lawn at the time of the garden's restoration.

A further modification in the trees of the Saarinen House garden took place when a large spruce by the side of the house was cut down. A protruding stump was left, marking its location. Earlier photos show the young tree fit well in its place. But as the spruce grew, it began to overflow its bed and eventually overwhelmed the side of the house. Its removal many years ago, along with the recent removal of the numerous *Lonicera* that had come up as volunteers in the area around it, allowed the lines of the house to become visible again.

The Restoration

Our work on the Saarinen House garden started with my research on the garden in the fall of 1992. My work on the site began in the spring of 1993. Patricia Crow, a member of my office, and the design-build landscape firm of Sandra Ahlers in Birmingham, Michigan, were soon able to begin work on site. Landscape contractor Marvin Niebauer of Rochester Tree and Landscaping in Oakland, Michigan, and irrigation consultant Russ May, also from Birmingham, Michigan, completed the team by the summer of 1993. The bulk of the work was finished by October of 1993. During spring of 1994 more overgrown shrubs were pruned and some hollyhocks were planted in the rear garden.[14] The search continued for the smaller spruce, *Picea orientalis* 'Gracilis,' which was chosen to replace the original but was unavailable at the time of planting. The *Picea omorika* in the color photographs was planted as a stopgap measure.

The following section by Patricia Crow will serve as a record of what was found on the site in the spring and summer of 1993 and what was restored between August of 1993 and summer of 1994. Unlike architecture, the installation of a landscape does not immediately produce a finished product. It will take five years to achieve the spatial effects intended for the garden, and even then the garden will not be finished, for its plants will continue to grow, mature, and die and will need replacement. The large trees, the elms, will effect the most dramatic transformation of the site, and it will be another fifteen years before they achieve the beautiful, curved, high-branching profile that is the enduring and unique mark of this tree.

Figure 53
Saarinen House, Lower Garden, with elm tree, during a party for students.
May 11, 1946

SAARINEN HOUSE GARDEN BEFORE AND AFTER

Patricia Crow

Finding the 1930s Garden

A garden restoration is made simpler when it is possible to use a combination of resources to discover the old garden. The Saarinen House garden was created recently enough that a number of such resources were available. Even with the somewhat disabling lack of an annotated planting plan of the original garden, it was possible to combine information several of sources to make reasonable deductions about the late 1930s period to which the garden has been restored.

An early planting scheme exists that indicates the Saarinens participated in the design of the garden. It is drawn on a sheet that includes the floor plan of the house (see Wittkopp, fig. 6). Inclusion of the floor plan in the drawing of a garden plan is unusual even today, and Platt did not do this in his planting schemes for Cranbrook. Not only is the drawing in Eliel's hand, but the planting sensibility is different from Platt's. This is the only location at Cranbrook where a formal hedge—the barberry mentioned earlier—is used as the framework of the garden. It seems likely that the Saarinens had ideas for the garden framework, and that Platt was brought in to fill it out.

A survey of existing conditions in May of 1993 showed a garden that had outgrown its space and lost its intended form. Self-seeded honeysuckles and old dogwoods in need of pruning sat among stumps that should have been removed years before. The age of some of these plants indicated that they may have been original, but they were beyond pruning back to a size and shape that were in scale with the garden space. It was decided to take a careful inventory and to compare what was existing with old photographs and other material found in the Cranbrook Archives to determine the next step.

Platt's planting plans for other areas at Cranbrook allowed us to identify with some precision the old plants in the Saarinen garden. In most cases, the species was recognizable from old photographs, and the lists of plants culled from Platt's old plans provided the likely cultivar. The remnant stumps in the garden gave exact locations for the original trees.

Where original plant material was healthy and could be pruned over time back to manageable size, we decided, with Gregory Wittkopp, curator for the house's restoration, to keep it, even though an awkward stage would have to be passed through before the ideal size and shape were achieved. All material that was not part of the 1930s planting was removed. New planting would employ the same cultivars that were planted initially. Even though improved cultivars have become available, we decided to stay with the original where possible. Where the same cultivar could not be found, a substitution was made with the understanding that the search would continue for the desired plant.

Sometimes it was impossible to identify the original shrub. In these cases, we chose a plant that we know Platt used and that resembled the original shrub pictured in the photographs. (See lists of existing plants and new planting on page 161.)

With the exception of the ivy and barberry, most of the plant material used originally in the Saarinen House garden was also used in the garden of the headmaster's residence across the street. Pink or white spring flowers, red and bronze fall-leaf color, and fragrance are characteristic of many of the plantings in the garden. Shrub borders had a simple cut edge where they met the lawn, and apparently were not mulched and not usually underplanted with groundcover. (See plant list for headmaster's residence on page 161.)

Restoration of Planting

Framework

If there was an element that unified the Saarinen
House garden with the other gardens along
Academy Way facing the Triton Pool, it was the common rear-garden wall with the elm trees arching
above, which was perceived from the mall as a
straight row of trees fairly regularly spaced (fig. 54).
The two essential elements in the Saarinen House
garden that set it apart from the rest of the
Cranbrook campus were the eighteen-inch-high
barberry hedge that gave structure to the planting
areas, and the use of the brick walls as a framework
for vines to integrate the house and the garden. The
original *Berberis thunbergii* hedge had been
replaced in the side garden by *Ligustrum* and in the
rear garden by *Ilex crenata.* We replaced these with
Berberis hedge, to bring once again to the garden
the ribbon of red fall color of the Saarinens' time.
The search for simple *Berberis thunbergii* with its red
fruit, tender green leaves, and good fall color was
complicated by the many new types on the market.
They are thought to be preferable but vary enough
to be a questionable choice for this garden
restoration.

An abundance of existing *Parthenocissus tricuspidata*
on the building walls brought only the question of
how much to remove. The simultaneous restoration
of the window frames of the building required the
removal of much of this plant. As it grows back, we
hope that a balance can be maintained between
plant and building so that the brick patterns can continue to be appreciated in summer as well as in
winter. Together the intricate patterns of the brick
and the tender *Parthenocissus*
branching create a meaning-
ful texture.

The other ivy on the site, a
birds' foot *Hedera helix,* had
migrated from the north-
facing studio wall to the east
side of the building, where it
climbed up the gable and
onto the roof tiles. We
returned the ivy to its original
location as an evergreen
frame for the sculpture
niches on the north-facing
studio wall. Here the building wall, already rich with
its patterning of brick, acts as a garden wall that is an
armature for ceramic vases and for the two types of
ivy (fig. 55).

Across the octagon courtyard, on the columns that
form the edge of the porch, single stems of

157

Parthenocissus had been trained to climb the center of the columns. These columns had metal hooks embedded in the mortar near the top. It is unclear whether the ivy was trained on wires fastened to these hooks. This method would have been similar to that used to train the Dorothy Perkins roses on the front retaining wall on Academy Way. We replanted *Parthenocissus* at the base of the columns with the intention of training them as a single-stem espalier.

Front Garden

In the front garden by the door the two *Taxus* were replaced. Each was of a different species and had been so badly pruned over the years as to make symmetrical forms impossible. A doorway or pathway marked by a matched pair of evergreen shrubs was a device that Platt frequently employed at Cranbrook, and he used it again to mark thresholds here and elsewhere in the Saarinen House garden.

As mentioned, old photographs show that the front wall of the Saarinen House garden and the adjacent Milles House garden had a continuous collar of Dorothy Perkins roses supported by a frame fashioned from metal hooks and wires (fig. 56). The canes were behind the wall in the shade, and the blossoms opened to the afternoon sun along the sidewalk at shoulder height of the passer-by, their fragrance released by the warm sun. However, over the years most of the Dorothy Perkins roses in the Saarinen front garden had been replaced by other types of roses. We replanted a continuous line of these old-fashioned roses in their original location.

It is probable that the two Father Hugo roses planted at either side of the front steps are original. These are two of the shrubs that will take some time to prune back to a manageable form, but they can recover. The *Spiraea, Weigela,* and star magnolia remain. Cranbrook is no exception to the general rule in landscape design of planting campuses with shrubs, trees, and flowers that will bloom up to graduation time in mid-May.

Side Garden

As stated above, within the boundaries of the barberry hedge, the spruce had grown to dwarf the chimney it analogized and was cut down some years ago. In its place we have planted *Picea omorika,* but this will be replaced with *Picea orientalis* 'Gracilis' as soon as we find one. The latter has an ultimate columnar height of twenty feet and will remain in scale with the garden and the chimney. The honeysuckles and lilacs that had invaded all available space were beyond pruning and were removed, which made the delicate window and brick patterning and chimney details visible again. In an effort to save valuable existing trees, the pink and white dogwoods, which are so beautiful against the brick, have been pruned and treated for disease, and we hope they will survive.

In the side garden and across the walkway next to the architecture building, we replanted many old-fashioned shrubs typical of the 1930s, such as honeysuckles, *Deutzia, Spiraea,* mockorange, and black jetbead. Either side of the walkway is marked by a mugho pine. This route leads to the entrance to the lower part of the Saarinen House garden and to the mall.

Figure 56

Milles House, with Dorothy Perkins roses trained on the front wall. Photographed 1953

Rear Garden

As in the 1930s, two new pyramidal yews, *Taxus cuspidata* 'Capitata,' placed at the dining room doors have been shaved like cones. Two yews have been replanted at the door to the studio as well. Thus, each doorway is marked by Platt's device of an evergreen pair.

In the courtyard flowers are confined within the geometry of the barberry hedge or the paving. Tulips and anemones rise from behind the hedge at the studio windows. Mountain phlox surrounds the base of the sculpture in the center of the courtyard, and we have planted single hollyhocks, used in the Saarinens' time, on the sunny side.

Given the emphasis on spring-flowering shrubs, it would be easy to overlook the attention given to planting for the autumn months. Dramatic color change to red and burgundy favors the color of the brick and is accomplished by the existing winged Euonymus and Boston ivy, and the restoration of the barberry hedge and the *Viburnum* at the north side of the courtyard.

The three American Liberty elms we used to replace the ones lost in the 1970s had been held for years by the Municipal Nursery in Roseville, Michigan. The Elm Research Institute of Harrisville, New Hampshire, which has promoted reintroduction of a disease-resistant strain of American elms to the public landscape, brought the nursery to our attention as a possible source for the elms. Unfortunately, not enough of these elms were available to plant Academy Way as well. The street has been planted with Delaware II elms from Princeton Nurseries of New Jersey. Delaware II is also a disease-resistant cultivar and is a close relative of the American Liberty elm.

Remnants of the hook and wire system for training vines were found on the rear garden wall (fig. 57). Here, careful attention to pruning existing grape, wisteria, autumn flowering clematis, and Boston ivy will assure continuation of the theme of planted walls at this end of the garden.

Conclusion

The plan of the Saarinen House garden as restored includes a key showing which plants are thought to be original and which have been planted as part of the restoration (fig. 58). The availability of older cultivars has been less than satisfactory. This may be in part because interest in historic landscape and gardens is relatively new in the United States. A nationwide search provided no growers of some plants that were key to the restoration of the garden, for example, some of the honeysuckles. The commercial market is driven by convenience and low maintenance. In addition, the sense among many professionals and amateurs alike that the value of a shrub lies in the number or showiness of its flowers tends to create a market in which the shyer plants are overlooked and eventually are no longer grown commercially. The Saarinen House garden could have suffered from this preference had appropriate plant material not been available on the site. Keepers of the older cultivars are often garden club members or institutions such as botanical gardens and campuses. Thus, gardens like those at Cranbrook can become valuable sources for some of the older plants that have thrived there but are now commercially unavailable. More widespread interest in historic American landscapes is generated by such projects as the restoration of Saarinen House and its garden. As a result, continued cultivation of historic plant material may be assured, along with a more complete appreciation of the development of landscape architecture in this country.

Figure 57
Saarinen House, Courtyard, view of hook embedded in mortar to support wire. Photographed 1993

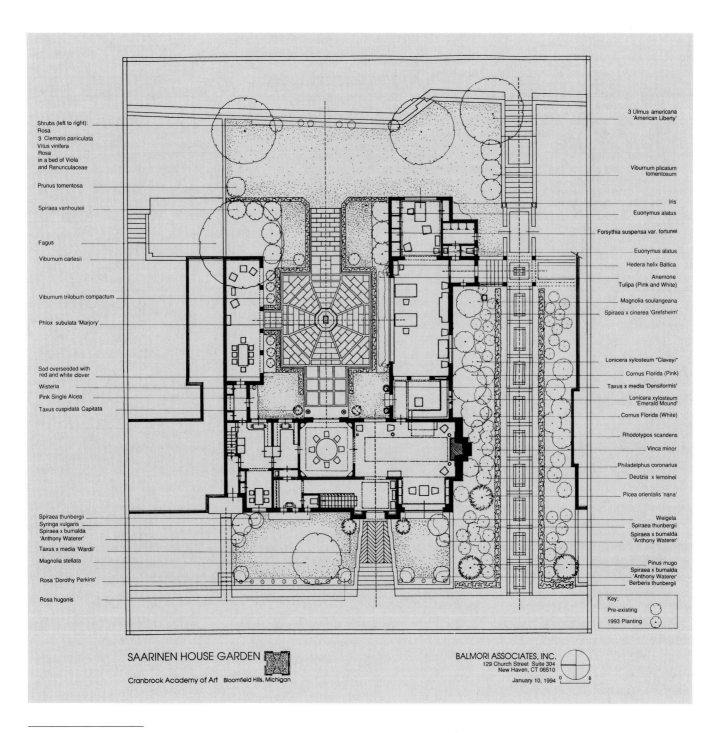

Shrubs (left to right):
Rosa
3 Clematis paniculata
Vitus vinifera
Rosa
in a bed of Viola
and Ranunculaceae

Prunus tomentosa

Spiraea vanhouteii

Fagus

Viburnum carlesii

Viburnum trilobum compactum

Phlox subulata 'Marjory'

Sod overseeded with
red and white clover

Wisteria

Pink Single Alcea

Taxus cuspidata Capitata

Spiraea thunbergii
Syringa vulgaris
Spiraea x bumalda
'Anthony Waterer'

Taxus x media 'Wardi'

Magnolia stellata

Rosa 'Dorothy Perkins'

Rosa hugonis

3 Ulmus americana
'American Liberty'

Viburnum plicatum
tomentosum

Iris
Euonymus alatus

Forsythia suspensa var. fortunei

Euonymus alatus

Hedera helix Baltica

Anemone
Tulipa (Pink and White)

Magnolia soulangeana

Spiraea x cinerea 'Grefsheim'

Lonicera xylosteum "Claveyi"

Cornus Florida (Pink)

Taxus x media 'Densiformis'

Lonicera xylosteum
'Emerald Mound'

Cornus Florida (White)

Rhodotypos scandens

Vinca minor

Philadelphus coronarius

Deutzia x lemoinei

Picea orientalis 'nana'

Weigela

Spiraea thunbergii

Spiraea x bumalda
'Anthony Waterer'

Pinus mugo

Spiraea x bumalda
'Anthony Waterer'
Berberis thunbergii

Key:

Pre-existing

1993 Planting

SAARINEN HOUSE GARDEN

Cranbrook Academy of Art   Bloomfield Hills, Michigan

BALMORI ASSOCIATES, INC.
129 Church Street Suite 304
New Haven, CT 06510

January 10, 1994

0   8

Figure 58

Saarinen House Garden as
restored, Plan. Drawing by
Patricia Crow, 1994, based
on plan by Eliel Saarinen

SAARINEN HOUSE GARDEN EXISTING CONDITIONS PLANT LIST MAY 1993

Front garden

Aegopodium podagraria •
1 *Deutzia gracilis*
1 *Ligustrum* •
1 *Lonicera morrowii*
1 *Magnolia stellata*
Rosa •
2 *Rosa hugonis**
1 *Spiraea thunbergii**
1 *Spiraea vanhouttei**
5 *Spiraea x bumalda* 'Anthony Waterer' *
1 *Syringa vulgaris* •
1 *Taxus cuspidata* •
1 *Taxus x media* 'Wardii' •
1 *Weigela florida*

Side Garden

2 *Cornus florida* (one pink, one white)*
Ligustrum (hedge) •
5 *Lonicera tatarica* •
2 *Spiraea x vanhouttei* •
5 *Syringa vulgaris* •

Rear Garden

Anemones
4 *Azalea* •
1 *Buxus sempervirens* •
2 *Clematis paniculata**
4 *Euonymus alatus* (one kept and pruned)* •
1 *Fagus sylvatica*
1 *Forsythia x intermedia**
Hedera helix*
Ilex crenata (hedge) •
Iris
3 *Lonicera tatarica* •
Pachysandra terminalis
Paeonies •
Parthenocissus tricuspidata*

1 *Prunus tomentosa**
3 *Spiraea* •
1 *Taxus cuspidata* 'Capitata' •
Tradescantia virginiana •
Vinca minor
1 *Vitus vinifera**
1 *Wisteria sinensis**

  • Removed or replaced
  * Pruned

SAARINEN HOUSE GARDEN NEW PLANTING AUGUST 1993

206 *Berberis thunbergii*

Front garden

12 *Rosa* Dorothy Perkins
1 *Spiraea x bumalda* 'Anthony Waterer'
1 *Syringa vulgaris*
2 *Taxus cuspidata*

Side garden

3 *Deutzia x lemoinei*
2 *Lonicera xylosteum* 'Claveyi' (while waiting for *Lonicera tatarica*)
3 *Lonicera xylosteum* 'Emerald Mound' (while waiting for *Lonicera morrowii*)
1 *Magnolia x soulangeana*
1 *Philadelphus coronarius*
1 *Picea omorika* (while waiting for *orientalis* 'Gracilis')
2 Mugho pine
6 *Rhodotypos scandens* (syn. *kerrioides*)
11 *Spiraea thunbergii*
9 *Spiraea x cinerea* 'Grefsheim'
Vinca minor

Rear Garden

Alcea (single pink)
1 *Euonymus alatus*
Grass seed and sod overseeded with red and white clover
40 *Phlox subulata* 'Marjory'
14 *Spiraea x vanhouttei*
2 *Taxus cuspidata* 'Capitata'
2 *Taxus x media* 'Densiformis'
Tulipa (pink and white)
3 *Ulmus americana* 'American Liberty'
2 *Viburnum carlesii*
3 *Viburnum plicatum* var. *tomentosum*
6 *Viburnum trilobum* 'Compactum'

C. DEFOREST PLATT'S PLANT LIST FOR HEADMASTER'S RESIDENCE**

Front

Acer ginnala
Clematis paniculata
Elm
3 Flowering almond
6 *Forsythia suspensa* var. *fortunei*
Lonicera tatarica Rosea
Malus baccata
Philadelphus coronarius
Philadelphus virginalis
Rhodotypos kerriodes
Rosa
Syringa
Viburnum plicatum tomentosum

Side

Acer saccharum
Large lilacs
Lonicera maacki
Lonicera tatarica Rosea
Syringa japonica
Viburnum tomentosum
Wisteria sinensis

Back

Acer saccharum
4 *Amelanchier laevis*
10 *Aronia arbutifolia*
Bachtels crab
Betula alba
Cladrastis lutea
Cornus florida
Devil's can
Elm
2 *Euonymus alatus*
5 Flowering almond
2 Large mugho pine
8 Ligustrum
11 *Ligustrum ibota*
3 *Ligustrum regeliarnum*
5 *Lonicera bella rosea*
6 *Lonicera fragrantissima*
Lonicera kerakowi
19 *Lonicera maacki*
5 *Lonicera morrowii*
Malus baccata
4 Mugho pine
Parkman's crab
Perennials such as iris, peonies, phlox, helenium
3 *Pinus montana*
9 *Pinus sylvestris*
5 *Prunus glandulosa*
Prunus subhirtella
Quercus rubra
7 Regel privet
14 *Spiraea thunbergii*
10 *Symphoricarpos racemosa*

  ** Also called the Art Director's Residence and now two academy faculty residences

NOTES

Slade

1. Albert Christ-Janer, *Eliel Saarinen: Finnish-American Architect and Educator,* foreword by Alvar Aalto, rev. ed. (Chicago: The University of Chicago Press, 1979), 87-88.

2. Arthur Pound, *The Only Thing Worth Finding: The Life and Legacies of George Gough Booth* (Detroit: Wayne State University Press, 1964), 482.

Wittkopp

1. Eliel Saarinen, *The City: Its Growth, Its Decay, Its Future* (New York: Reinhold, 1943), 18.

2. See, for example, Henry P. Macomber, "The Michigan Home of Eliel Saarinen," *House Beautiful* 74 (October 1933), 133-36.

3. For a discussion of the house as it appeared after it was refurbished in the late 1970s, see Peter C. Papademetriou, "Eliel Saarinen," *Global Architecture Houses* 9 (July 1981), 8-19.

4. From 1988 through 1994, the author was responsible for researching and supervising all aspects of the restoration of the structure and interiors. Diana Balmori researched the restoration of the garden, the subject of the second essay in this book.

5. The majority of the architectural drawings are in the collection of the Cranbrook Archives; additional drawings are in the collection of Cranbrook Academy of Art Museum and the Museum of Finnish Architecture, Helsinki. Hereafter, Cranbrook Academy of Art Museum will be abbreviated "CAAM."

6. Most of the historic photographs are in the collections of the Cranbrook Archives, CAAM, and Ronald Saarinen Swanson, a grandson of Eliel and Loja.

7. Cranbrook Archives, Cranbrook Architectural Office Files, accession number 1989-1. Hereafter, this collection will be abbreviated "CAOF, 1989-1."

8. Cranbrook Archives, George Gough Booth Papers, accession number 1981-1. Hereafter, this collection will be abbreviated "GGBP, 1981-1."

9. Cranbrook Archives, Saarinen Family Papers, accession number 1990-08. Hereafter, this collection will be abbreviated "SFP, 1990-08."

10. This file was transferred from the administration offices to the art museum in 1994. "Cranbrook Academy of Art: Inventories of Furnishings," CAAM, Saarinen House Research Files. Hereafter, these research files will be abbreviated "SHRF."

11. Cranbrook Archives, SFP, 1990-08, box 3, folder 1.

12. Reports from Frank Welsh to Gregory Wittkopp, June 1, 1988, through December 20, 1993, CAAM, SHRF.

13. Paul Goldberger, "Bringing Back Saarinen," *The New York Times Magazine,* April 16, 1978, 92 ff.

14. Richard Guy Wilson, "Architecture in the Machine Age," in Richard Guy Wilson et al., *The Machine Age in America, 1918-1941* (New York: Harry N. Abrams, 1986), 149.

15. "Address of George Howe," in *Contemporary Architecture: A Symposium Presented at the Sixty-Third Convention of The American Institute of Architects, Washington, D.C., May 21, 22, 23, 1930,* 5-8. This transcript of the symposium was distributed by the Committee on Education of the American Institute of Architects.

16. "Address of C. Howard Walker," in ibid., 11.

17. Ibid., 13-14.

18. Henry-Russell Hitchcock Jr. and Philip Johnson, *The International Style: Architecture Since 1922* (New York: W. W. Norton and Company, 1932). Of the American architects noted above, George Howe is the only one included in this publication.

19. "Cranbrook Academy of Art, Bloomfield Hills, Michigan," *The Architectural Record* 68 (December 1930), 444-51.

20. The program of the competition, report of the jury, and illustrations of the submitted designs were published as *The International Competition for a New Administration Building for the Chicago Tribune MCMXXII* (Chicago: The Tribune Company, 1923).

21. George C. Nimmons, "Skyscrapers in America," *The Journal of the American Institute of Architects* 11 (September 1923), 370-72.

22. Dr. Ing. Walter Curt Behrendt, "Skyscrapers in Germany," in ibid., 365-70.

23. *The International Competition,* 5.

24. Dorothy Nyberg Carlson remembers her mother, Gerda Nyberg, one of the Saarinens' housekeepers, telling her about a dinner that she served at Saarinen House to the "winning architects of the Chicago Tribune Tower competition." One of the guests mentioned that if Eliel had been an American, he would have won the competition. Dorothy Nyberg Carlson, telephone conversation with the author, December 6, 1993, CAAM, SHRF.

25. The fact that John Mead Howell's wife, Abby White, was a daughter of an early editor of the *Tribune* also may have influenced the decision. "The key to the *Tribune*'s management," *Fortune* 9 (May 1934), 108.

26. *The International Competition,* 7.

27. Irving K. Pond, "High Buildings and Beauty," *The Architectural Forum* 38 (February 1923), 42.

28. Thomas E. Tallmadge, *The Story of Architecture in America* (New York: W. W. Norton and Company, 1936), 292.

29. Louis H. Sullivan, "The Chicago Tribune Competition," *The Architectural Record* 53 (February 1923), 153.

30. Francisco Mujica, *History of the Skyscraper* (Paris: Archaeology and Architecture Press, 1929, reprint, New York: Da Capo Press, 1977), 62.

31. Claude Bragdon, *The Frozen Fountain: Being Essays on Architecture and the Art of Design in Space* (New York: Alfred A. Knopf, 1932), 32.

32. Raymond Hood, "The American Radiator Company Building, New York," *The American Architect and Architectural Review* 126 (November 19, 1924), 466-74.

33. Loja Saarinen to J. S. Siren, July 16, 1955, Cranbrook Archives, SFP, 1990-08, box 1, folder 3.

34. The only comprehensive biography of Saarinen's career is Albert Christ-Janer, *Eliel Saarinen: Finnish-American Architect and Educator,* foreword by Alvar Aalto, rev. ed. (Chicago: The University of Chicago Press, 1979). For the most recent study of his career in Finland see Marika Hausen et al., *Eliel Saarinen: Projects, 1896-1923* (Cambridge: The MIT Press, 1990).

35. Juhani Pallasmaa, ed., *Hvitträsk: Koti Taideteoksena/The Home as a Work of Art* (Helsinki: Suomen Rakennustaiteen Museo/Museum of Finnish Architecture, 1987).

36. The most detailed discussion of the Helsinki Railway Station is in Marika Hausen, "The Helsinki Railway Station in Eliel Saarinen's first version 1904," *Taidehistoriallisia Tutkimuksia - Konsthistoriska Studier* 3 (1977), 57-114. See also Gregory Wittkopp, "Railway Station and Administrative Building, Helsinki, Finland," in *International Dictionary of Architects and Architecture* 2, Architecture (Detroit: St. James Press, 1993), 170-71.

37. Eliel Saarinen, *The City.* For a discussion of Saarinen's work as a city planner, see Marc Treib, "Urban Fabric by the Bolt: Eliel Saarinen at Munkkiniemi-Haaga, *Architectural Association Quarterly* 2-3 (1982), 42-58.

38. Christ-Janer, *Eliel Saarinen,* 59.

39. Tytti Valto, "Catalogue of Works," in Marika Hausen et al., *Eliel Saarinen: Projects,* 335. Strengell was one of the architects who had criticized Saarinen's first design for the Helsinki Railway Station. In 1937 his daughter, Marianne, started teaching at Cranbrook and in 1942 followed Loja as head of the Department of Weaving and Textile Design.

40. Emil Lorch, "Tendencies in High Building Design," *The Michigan Daily,* March 18, 1923, 3 ff., Cranbrook Archives, SFP, 1990-08, box 1, folder 2.

41. Emil Lorch to George Booth, April 28, 1923, Cranbrook Archives, GGBP, 1981-1, box 13, folder 11.

42. The University of Michigan, for example, notes that Eliel was at the college less than five months, through March 1924. Jeanelle Richardson, College Recorder, College of Architecture and Urban Planning, University of Michigan, to Chiyo Ishikawa, August 21, 1981, Cranbrook Archives, SFP, 1990-08, box 1, folder 1.

43. Emil Lorch, "Annual Report of the College of Architecture for Year 1925-26," Cranbrook Archives, GGBP, 1981-1, box 13, folder 13.

44. Emil Lorch to George Booth, February 16, 1925, Cranbrook Archives, GGBP, 1981-1, box 13, folder 13.

45. Today, the community includes Cranbrook Schools, Cranbrook Institute of Science, and Cranbrook Academy of Art and Cranbrook Academy of Art Museum.

46. Arthur Pound, *The Only Thing Worth Finding: The Life and Legacies of George Gough Booth* (Detroit: Wayne State University Press, 1964).

47. Christ-Janer, *Eliel Saarinen,* 65.

48. Albert Kahn to George Booth, August 27, 1942, Cranbrook Archives, GGBP, 1981-1, box 16, folder 21.

49. Booth's remarks were made in 1942 at Cranbrook during ceremonies wherein he was made an honorary member of the American Institute of Architects. Mark Coir (Director, Cranbrook Archives), conversation with the author, March 8, 1994.

50. Program titled "Architecture: Eliel Saarinen," Cranbrook Archives, SFP, 1990-08, box 1, folder 1.

51. Davira S. Taragin, "The History of the Cranbrook Community," in Robert Judson Clark et al., *Design in America: The Cranbrook Vision, 1925-1950* (New York: Harry N. Abrams, 1983), 38.

52. George Booth to Eliel Saarinen, October 6, 1924, Cranbrook Archives, SFP, 1990-08, box 2, folder 12.

53. I am indebted to Mark Coir for his insights on the development of Cranbrook, including the important roles played by George Booth, Henry Booth, and J. Robert F. Swanson. For the only published account of this interpretation, see Mark Coir, "School Opens As Farm Buildings Turn Into Classrooms and Dorms," *Cranbrook Kingswood Tradition* 3 (Spring 1991), 19. In addition, see Mark Coir, "George Gough Booth and the Planning of Cranbrook" (unpublished manuscript, Wayne State University, 1992).

54. Swanson graduated in 1925. Cranbrook Archives, SFP, 1990-08, box 1, folder 1.

55. Henry S. Booth, interview by Mary Riordan, Davira Tarigan, and John Gerard, September 10, 1979, and J. Robert F. Swanson, interview by Davira Tarigan and John Gerard, February 7, 1980, CAAM.

56. J. Robert F. Swanson, interview, CAAM.

57. Cranbrook Archives, Records of the Board of Trustees (Series I), accession number 1990-3, box 1.

58. Mary Beth Kreiner, "Introduction to Index," Cranbrook Archives, CAOF, 1989-1.

59. Prior to living in this residence, the Saarinens stayed for a few weeks in another house, a former farm building on the site of the Beresford property on Lone Pine Road. Mark Coir, conversation with the author, March 9, 1994.

60. The Saarinens lived in the farmhouse next to the main pedestrian entrance to the boys' school.

61. The exact year they moved to the Swansons' home is not known. J. Robert F. Swanson, interview, CAAM.

62. These plans are discussed by John Gerard, "Research on the Master Plan for CAA," unpublished manuscript, CAAM, Saarinen Research Files.

63. Cranbrook Archives, Records of the Board of Trustees (Series I), accession number 1990-3, box 1.

64. Cranbrook Archives, accession numbers AD.11.101-108.

65. Cranbrook Archives, CAOF, 1989-1, box 12, folder 17.

66. Ibid.

67. Cranbrook Archives, CAOF, 1989-1, box 12, folders 17-18.

68. *The Detroit News*, September 14, 1930, part 6, p. 2. This is the same edition in which the first article on Saarinen House appeared: Florence Davies, "Here, Logic and Beauty are United," *The Detroit News*, September 14, 1930.

69. Cranbrook Archives, CAOF, 1989-1, box 12, folder 19.

70. Ibid., box 13, folder 1.

71. Davies, "Here, Logic and Beauty are United."

72. Henry Booth designed the stone plaque with "Saarinen House" carved in relief that was installed to the right of the front door. In a discussion with the author on March 9, 1994, Mark Coir noted that this was probably done in the early 1950s shortly after Eliel's death.

73. Davies, "Here, Logic and Beauty are United."

74. The "Brittany Shingle" clay tiles were manufactured by the Ludowici-Celadon Company, Chicago. Cranbrook Archives, CAOF, 1989-1, box 13, folder 4.

75. The wood trim around the metal window sashes was finished with a pigmented oil varnish, not a stain. Report from Frank Welsh to Gregory Wittkopp, July 19, 1993, CAAM, SHRF.

76. Accession number AD.11.585. For the stop and stool of the mirror, the drawing simply specifies "special wood to match furniture." Macassar ebony was used in the restoration for both the stop and stool to match the veneers on the table below the mirror. It is not clear, however, whether the table as well as the other veneered furniture in the front hall, living room, and book room has Macassar ebony or rosewood veneers.

77. Although two "stools" and one "bench" "by Berglund" are noted on Loja's 1950 inventory, the location of the upholstered "stools" is not known. The current upholstered benches are reproductions based on a comparison of the surviving table (CAAM, accession number 1977.4) and a historic photograph.

78. The rug is documented by just one period photograph (see fig. 9). As it is not noted on Loja's inventory, it is assumed to have worn out and have been discarded by the Saarinens. The reproduction was woven on a surviving Cranbrook Loom, which was designed by Loja Saarinen.

79. This comparison was suggested by Thomas Trombley, to whom I am indebted for his many valuable insights and interpretations. For a discussion of hallstands, see Kenneth L. Ames, "Meaning in Artifacts: Hall Furnishings in Victorian America," in *Material Culture Studies in America*, compiled and ed. Thomas J. Schlereth (Nashville: AASLH Press, 1982), 213.

80. Although the globe stand does not appear in any of the historic photographs of Saarinen House, its presence in this location has been noted by the Saarinens' grandchildren, Robert Saarinen Swanson and Ronald Saarinen Swanson, during several conversations with the author. This view is supported by the use of rosewood or Macassar ebony veneers on the globe stand, which match the veneers used on the other furniture in the room.

81. For a discussion of the work of Eliel Saarinen within the context of contemporary designers such as Paul Frankl, see Karen Davies, *At Home in Manhattan: Modern Decorative Arts, 1925 to the Depression* (New Haven: Yale University Art Gallery, 1983).

82. CAAM, accession numbers 1928.39 and 1982.98, respectively.

83. Davies, "Here, Logic and Beauty are United."

84. See *The Architect and the Industrial Arts: An Exhibition of Contemporary American Design*, exh. cat. (New York: The Metropolitan Museum of Art, 1929), 61, and Macomber, "Michigan Home of Eliel Saarinen," 133.

85. Pewabic Society, Inc., Archives, Detroit, Michigan, research folder number 2-30. The color is noted on the back of an early photograph of the fireplace.

86. Ibid. A diagram of the original measurements (10 ft. 3 in. wide) appears on a handwritten draft for a letter from the Pewabic Pottery to Eliel Saarinen, January 15, 1930.

87. Davies, "Here, Logic and Beauty are United."

88. *The Architect and the Industrial Arts*, 61. J. David Farmer notes that "a newspaper article on the Cranbrook foundry [*Detroit News*, July 20, 1930] shows the Cranbrook smith Francis Faus polishing an identical andiron." However, given the fact that these andirons were executed prior to the February 1929 opening of the exhibition at the Metropolitan, it is likely that Faus was simply polishing the andirons to prepare for their

use in Saarinen House. See J. David Farmer, "Metalwork and Bookbinding," in *Design in America*, 163 and 315, note 43.

89. Henry S. Booth, interview, CAAM.

90. The best discussions of Loja's career remain Christa C. Mayer Thurman, "Textiles," in *Design in America*, 175-83, and John Gerard, *Studio Loja Saarinen*, exh. cat. (Bloomfield Hills: Cranbrook Academy of Art Museum, 1980).

91. For a detailed discussion of these textiles, now in the collection of The Victoria and Albert Museum, see Christopher Wilk, *The Kaufmann Office: Frank Lloyd Wright* (London: The Victoria and Albert Museum, 1993).

92. Davies, "Here, Logic and Beauty are United," and Macomber, "Michigan Home of Eliel Saarinen."

93. John Boulton Smith, *The Golden Age of Finnish Art* (Helsinki: Ministry for Foreign Affairs, 1975), 41.

94. Riitta Pylkkänen, *The Use and Traditions of Mediaeval Rugs and Coverlets in Finland* (Helsinki: Suomen Muinaismuistoyhdistys/Archaeological Society of Finland, 1974), 59.

95. For a further discussion of the furniture, see R. Craig Miller, "Interior Design and Furniture," in *Design in America*, 93-94.

96. Kersten Berglund Kavanagh (Berglund's daughter), telephone conversations with Mark Coir, November 2, 1993, and the author, February 7, 1994, Cranbrook Archives.

97. Cranbrook Archives, Records of the Board of Trustees (Series I), accession number 1990-3, box 1.

98. Aileen Ryan, "Furnish Home According to Principles of Architecture," *The Milwaukee Journal*, January 18, 1942, section 7, p. 9.

99. In a discussion with the author in 1993, Ronald Saarinen Swanson noted that the stone carving was documented in this location by a historic photograph in his collection. Unfortunately, the photograph is now missing.

100. Two different pedestals appear in the historic photographs. The simpler one that appears in the 1930 photographs is later replaced by a veneered pedestal made by Tor Berglund. Cranbrook Archives, Cranbrook Academy of Art, "Crafts Shops Inventory 1929-1933," accession number 1982-7.

101. Macomber, "Michigan Home of Eliel Saarinen," 136.

102. Report from Frank Welsh to Gregory Wittkopp, July 25, 1991, CAAM, SHRF.

103. Kirmo Mikkola, "Eliel Saarinen and Town Planning," in Marika Hausen et al., *Eliel Saarinen: Projects*, 191.

104. Anna Danielson, telephone conversation with the author, January 5, 1994, CAAM, SHRF. Danielson was the Saarinens' housekeeper during the 1930s.

105. The gray stain was achieved by wiping the wood with a black stain followed by a white pigment and

damar varnish. Report from Frank Welsh to Gregory Wittkopp, May 17, 1990, CAAM, SHRF.

106. The curtains used in the restoration are reproductions based on a historic photograph (see fig. 13). Their color was determined by matching the tan and rust in the upholstery on the nearby lounge chairs. A close examination of fig. 19 shows that the same curtains were also used on the window behind the globe stand.

107. Viktor Schreckengost to Loja Saarinen, March 19, 1938, Cranbrook Archives, SFP, 1990-08, box 2, folder 7. Unfortunately, no correspondence or invoices survive for the other objects in the book room.

108. Macomber, "Michigan Home of Eliel Saarinen," 136.

109. R. L. Fulton to Cranbrook Architectural Office, May 8, 1930, Cranbrook Archives, CAOF, 1989-1, box 1, folder 11.

110. Ibid., Cranbrook Architectural Office to C. R. Wermuth & Son, Inc., May 9, 1930.

111. The base and crown moldings had been covered with several layers of white paint while the niches survived intact, with the exception of their face moldings, under the wallboard.

112. Report from Frank Welsh to Gregory Wittkopp, May 17, 1990, CAAM, SHRF.

113. The new finish, formulated by Lawrence McLoskey of A Notch Above, uses lime to bleach the wood followed by an application of pure beeswax.

114. For a discussion of the restoration of the twenty-three-karat gold leaf, see Gregory Wittkopp, "Saarinen House dining room restored to original beauty," *Cranbrook Journal* (Fall 1990), 2-3.

115. See, for example, Miller, "Interior Design," 95.

116. William Coffin to Eliel Saarinen, August 21, 1930, Cranbrook Archives, GGBP, 1981-1, box 19, folder 32.

117. The Saarinens' trips to Europe are documented in Christ-Janer, *Eliel Saarinen*, 135-38.

118. Rosemarie Haag Bletter, "The Art Deco Style," in *Skyscraper Style: Art Deco New York* (New York: Oxford University Press, 1975), 35.

119. Ibid., 71.

120. Ibid., 55.

121. For a discussion of this rug as well as other textiles in the house, see Thurman, "Textiles," *Design in America*, 177.

122. The exhibition opened at the Metropolitan on February 12, 1929, and, while not all of the furniture was finished for the opening, a picture in an undocumented newspaper clipping shows the rug in place. Cranbrook Archives, SFP, 1990-08, box 1, folder 2.

123. Alexander Tzonis visited Saarinen House with the author in January 1993.

124. Alexander Tzonis and Lione Lefaivre, *Architecture in Europe: Memory and Invention Since 1968* (New York: Rizzoli, 1992), 152-54.

125. Ryan, "Principles of Architecture."

126. The original side panels were rediscovered in 1992 in a locked closet in the basement under the original headmaster's residence on Academy Way. They were correctly identified by Thomas Trombley. The woven plaid curtains between the side panels and the doors are adaptations based on a historic photograph. However, the original fabric may have been a commercially printed, not a woven, fabric.

127. As recently as 1993, in Peter Barnet and MaryAnn Wilkinson, *Decorative Arts 1900: Highlights from Private Collections in Detroit*, exh. cat. (Detroit: The Detroit Institute of Arts, 1993), 100, this creamer and sugar bowl were attributed to Eliel Saarinen. Following a suggestion made by Martin Eidelberg, the author located the faint stamp of Eisenlöffel on top of the sugar-bowl lid.

128. According to Donald Jenkins, Curator of Asian Art, Portland Museum of Art, Oregon, the original print was a "surimono," a privately commissioned special-occasion print incorporating poems, dating from ca. 1810 to 1840, possibly by Hokusai (1760-1849). Donald Jenkins to David Rau, January 19, 1994, CAAM. The Japanese woodblock print used in the restoration was owned by Eliel and Loja, although it does not appear in any of the historic photographs.

129. Purchase Requisition for Academy Residence #1 from Charles Wermuth and Sons, May 23, 1930, Cranbrook Archives, CAOF, 1989-1, box 13, folder 9.

130. The open shelf on top of the refrigerator, which appears in fig. 17, was removed during the restoration. Although it was obviously added by the Saarinens, it was not part of the original conception of the pantry. The pantry also contains a pass-through to the kitchen added by the Paulsens in the 1960s.

131. One of the small tubular chairs may be the chair currently used in the studio with Eliel's desk, although the inventory also notes three tubular chairs in the living room and one rust tubular chair in the upper hallway.

132. Anna Danielson, telephone conversations with the author, March 29, 1993, December 20, 1993, and January 5, 1994.

133. For a reference to the dolls, see Margaret Fish, "Saarinen Cites Keynotes for City's War Memorial," *Milwaukee Sentinel* (ca. February 22, 1947). An undated copy of this article is at CAAM, SHRF.

134. See, for example, the inventory of the house that Loja compiled in 1950. Although the common spelling is "cozy," Loja preferred the variant with an "s."

135. Florence Davies, "The Weavings of Loja Saarinen," *The Weaver* 2 (January 1937), 14.

136. The color of the cushions is noted by Margaret Fish, "Saarinen Cites Keynotes," and by Pipsan Saarinen Swanson during an interview with John Gerard, September 6, 1977, CAAM, Saarinen Research File.

137. Anna-Lisa Amberg, "Catalogue of the Interiors in Eliel Saarinen's Home," in *Hvitträsk*, ed. Pallasmaa, 93.

138. There are three tables of similar overall geometric design, but with different center inlays: the one in the collection of CAAM, which has been used in the restoration, one in the collection of Ronald Saarinen Swanson (formerly in the collection of Dorothy Sepeshy), and one in a private collection. The one in the museum's collection is dated January 1931 and is not the table originally used in the house. (See fig. 22, first published in December 1930.) However, the legs on both of the other two tables have been trimmed about 5 1/2 in. and therefore are inappropriate for the restored space. "Furniture Research/Saarinen," CAAM, Saarinen Research Files.

139. The soft light proved to be too dim for the Sepeshys, who had the colored leaded glass in the doors replaced with clear unleaded glass. When the house was refurbished by Roy Slade, leaded glass matching the original pattern was installed in the windows. However, as the soft yellow and green glass proved difficult to locate, a mottled clear glass was used. One original panel remains in the lower right corner of the right hand door.

140. Christ-Janer, *Eliel Saarinen*, xv.

141. The present location of these three antique *ryijys* is not known. Although the two included in the current restoration are from Eliel's original collection, they do not appear in any of the historic photographs of the house.

142. Anna Danielson, telephone conversation with the author, January 5, 1994.

143. Invoice dated February 6, 1933, Cranbrook Archives, SFP, 1990-08, box 4, folder 5.

144. Henry Booth to Loja Saarinen, September 20, 1950, Cranbrook Archives, SFP, 1990-08, box 3, folder 1.

145. Fish, "Saarinen Cites Keynotes." The flat files were not reinstalled for the photographs in this book.

146. It appears that the doors to the three closets in the office alcove were also refinished at this time to match the lighter finish.

147. Fish, "Saarinen Cites Keynotes." The color of the curtains in the office alcove was not documented until after the current set of green curtains was woven and installed in 1988 based on a green set at CAAM (accession number ZO 1983 14 a-c). In June 1990 the author observed a yellow pair of the same design hanging in Hvitträsk in the bathroom off the children's playroom.

148. The color of this rug was noted by Margueritte Kimball in a telephone conversation with the author in 1993.

149. George Booth to Emil Lorch, May 5, 1926, Cranbrook Archives, GGBP, 1981-1, box 13, folder 14.

150. Louis G. Redstone, *Louis G. Redstone: From Israeli Pioneer to American Architect* (Ames: Iowa State University Press, 1989), 120.

151. Louis Redstone, conversation with the author, January 11, 1994.

152. Although the *ryijy* rug used in the restoration was from Eliel's collection, it does not appear in the historic photographs. We do not know the location of the original rugs.

153. Cranbrook Archives, Cranbrook Academy of Art Records, accession number 1982-7.

154. Anna Danielson, telephone conversation with the author, January 5, 1994. Danielson later visited Saarinen House with the author, on June 28, 1994. At that time she noted the bedspreads were slightly darker than those made for the restoration and had three rows of medium red piping along the top of the gathered sides. She also noted that the bedspreads should fold over the pillows rather than using shams.

155. Florence Davies, "The Changing Scene," *The Detroit News*, December 20, 1931.

156. Henry S. Booth, interview, CAAM.

157. The glass was supplied by the Vitrolite Construction Co. Cranbrook Archives, CAOF, 1989-1, box 12, folder 17.

158. The bed is in the collection of Anna Danielson. Its rounded headboard recalls the desk in the studio while the veneers and finish recall the credenza. Cranbrook Archives, Cranbrook Academy of Art, "Crafts Shops Inventory 1929-1933," accession number 1982-7.

159. Charles R. Wermuth and Son to Cranbrook Architectural Office, December 17, 1930, CAOF, 1989-1, box 13, folder 2.

160. Cranbrook Archives, CAOF, 1989-1, box 13, folder 1.

161. For a general account of the exhibition, which ran from November 5, 1934, to January 6, 1935, see "Contemporary American Industrial Art: 1934," *Bulletin of the Metropolitan Museum of Art* 29 (December 1934): 201, 203-05.

162. At an even later date, the enlarged room again was divided into two separate rooms retaining, however, the single entrance from the hallway. This is the current configuration of the rooms.

163. Christ-Janer, *Eliel Saarinen*, 21.

164. Ibid., 138.

165. Loja Saarinen to Henry Booth, September 13, 1951, Cranbrook Archives, SFP, 1990-08, box 3, folder 7.

166. Cranbrook Archives, accession number COM-508-4.

167. Invoice from Valentine Brotz Sons to Mrs. E. Saarinen, May 23, 1951, collection of Ronald Saarinen Swanson.

168. Glen Paulsen visited Saarinen House with the author on October 7, 1991. CAAM, SHRF.

169. Davies, "Here, Logic and Beauty are United."

170. Alvar Aalto, "Preface," in Christ-Janer, *Eliel Saarinen*, xiv.

171. Kenneth Reid, "Eliel Saarinen: Master of Design," *Pencil Points* 17 (September 1936), 481.

Balmori

1. Diana Balmori, "Architecture, Landscape, and the Intermediate Structure: Eighteenth-Century Experiments in Mediation," *Journal of the Society of Architectural Historians* 50 (March 1991), 38-56.

2. George G. Booth to Eliel Saarinen, "An Academy of Art at Cranbrook," 1925, Cranbrook Archives, George Gough Booth Papers (1908-25), accession number 1981-1, box 2, folder 4.

3. Robert Judson Clark et al., *Design in America: The Cranbrook Vision, 1925-1950* (New York: Harry N. Abrams, 1983).

4. Diana Balmori, "Cranbrook, The Invisible Landscape," *Journal of the Society of Architectural Historians* 53 (March 1994), 30-60.

5. William H. Whyte, *City* (New York: Doubleday, 1988).

6. Loja Saarinen to George Booth, July 29, 1942, Cranbrook Archives, George Gough Booth Papers, accession number 1981-1, box 19, folder 34.

7. Balmori, "Cranbrook: The Invisible Landscape," 30-60.

8. Interview with Dominick Vettraino, October 6, 1992. I am grateful to Mark Coir for several sources concerning Loja Saarinen's work and for the names of head gardeners and nurserymen from whom I could obtain oral accounts of Loja's work.

9. Interview with Marianne Strengell, October 20, 1993.

10. Anna Danielson, interview with Gregory Wittkopp, December 20, 1993.

11. Cranbrook Archives, Saarinen Family Papers, accession number 1990-08, box 3, folder 1. For documentation of her public role as a weaver, see Christa C. Mayer Thurman, "Textiles," in *Design in America*, 175-83, and John Gerard, *Studio Loja Saarinen*, exh. cat. (Bloomfield Hills: Cranbrook Academy of Art Museum, 1980).

12. Interview with Don Weber, October 27, 1993.

13. For information on Platt's work here, see "The Restoration of Fort Necessity," *Landscape Architecture* 22 (April 1932), 215, 217. (I would like to thank Diane Hilborn for the reference.)

14. A volunteer gardener at the Cranbrook Educational Community, Betty Trost, found a source for the hollyhocks.

Compiled by David D. J. Rau

*This list includes the names of the
principal people or companies affiliated with
the original construction of Saarinen House,
the objects used by the Saarinens, or the
restoration completed in 1994. The biogra-
phies focus on the affiliation with Cranbrook
and Saarinen House.*

*Cranbrook Academy of Art will be
abbreviated as "CAA."*

Wäinö Aaltonen
Born 1894, Karinainen, Finland; died 1966,
Helsinki, Finland

Hannes Autere
Born 1888, Saarijärvi, Finland; died 1967,
Saarijärvi

Barrymore Seamless Wiltons, Inc.
Incorporated 1921, Philadelphia,
Pennsylvania; closed

Christina Bechstein
Born 1968, Fort Wayne, Indiana; CAA stu-
dent, Department of Fiber, 1991–93,
M.F.A., 1993

Paula Stebbins Becker
Born 1961, Leominster, Massachusetts;
Jacquard textile designer, Craftex Mills,
Inc. of Penna. (see below), 1986-91; CAA
student, Department of Fiber, 1991–93,
M.F.A., 1993

Bentley Mills, Inc.
Established 1979, City of Industry,
California; currently in operation

Tor Berglund
Born 1879, Gavle, Sweden; head of the
Cabinet Shop, Cranbrook Arts and Crafts
Studios, 1929-32; died 1954, Hasselby,
Sweden

Harry Bertoia
Born 1915, San Lorenzo, Udine, Italy; CAA
student, Department of Metalworking,

1937; CAA metal craftsman, Department
of Metalworking, 1938–43; CAA faculty,
Department of Graphic Art, 1942–43;
died 1978, Barto, Pennsylvania

Henry Scripps Booth
Born 1897, Detroit, Michigan; University of
Michigan, School of Engineering, B. Arch.,
1924; partner in Swanson and Booth,
1924–26; office reorganized as Cranbrook
Architectural Office, 1926–50; private
practice called Henry S. Booth, Architect,
during the 1930s; primary architect at
Cranbrook Architectural Office,
1946–50; trustee of Cranbrook
Foundation, 1927–73; trustee of CAA,
1942–68; trustee of Brookside School,
1925–45; trustee of Cranbrook School for
boys, 1944–45; trustee of Kingswood
School for girls, 1944–45; director of
Kingswood School, 1930–43; vestryman of
Christ Church Cranbrook, 1942–44;
chairman and executive director,
Cranbrook Foundation, 1946–65; died
1988, Royal Oak, Michigan

Bradbury and Bradbury Art Wallpapers
Established 1979, Benicia, California;
currently in operation

Celeste Brush
Born 1953, Toronto, Canada; CAA student,
Department of Fiber, 1991–93, M.F.A.,
1993

Edward F. Caldwell and Company, Inc.
Established 1894, New York City, by
Edward F. Caldwell (born 1851; died 1914)
and Victor F. von Lossberg (see below);
liquidated 1957; reorganized by Edward
T. Caldwell, Jr.; closed 1959

Georgia Carroll
Born Georgia Finckel, 1905; active in
Michigan during the 1930s; married
painter John Carroll, 1936; died 1967

Chase Brass and Copper Company
Founded 1876, Waterbury, Connecticut;
closed in 1976

Christofle & Cie.
Founded 1830, Paris, France, by Joseph
Albert Bouilhet and Charles Christofle;
currently in operation

Collins and Aikman Corporation
Established 1843, New York City; current
headquarters in Charlotte, North Carolina

The Company of Master Craftsmen
The deluxe furniture division of W. and J.
Sloane, Flushing, Long Island, New York;
closed

Craftex Mills, Inc. of Penna.
Established 1920, Philadelphia,
Pennsylvania; current office in Blue Bell,
Pennsylvania, and weaving plant in Auburn,
Pennsylvania

Kay Dawson
Born 1956, Hutchinson, Kansas;
CAA student, Department of Fiber,
1980–82, M.F.A., 1982

Kristen Dettoni
Born 1969, Boston, Massachusetts; CAA
student, Department of Fiber, 1991–93,
M.F.A., 1993

Dominick & Haff
Established 1821 as William Gale & Son,
New York City; purchased by Reed &
Barton Silversmiths (see below), 1928

Elizabeth Edmark
Employed in the 1930s by Studio Loja
Saarinen (see below)

Olli Ehrström
Active in Helsinki, Finland, in the early
twentieth century

Jan Eisenlöffel
Born 1876, Amsterdam, the Netherlands; died 1957, Amsterdam

Enrico and Elenadi
Established ca. 1920, Scavini, Turin, Italy

Jean Eschmann
Born 1896, Basel, Switzerland; director of the Bookbinding Workshop, Cranbrook Arts and Crafts Studios, 1929–33; died 1961, Cleveland, Ohio

The Friends of Finnish Handicraft (Suomen Käsityön Ystävät Oy)
Founded 1879, Helsinki, Finland, by Fanny Churberg; currently in operation

Globe Dye Works Company
Established 1865, Philadelphia, Pennsylvania; currently in operation

A. B. Gustavsberg
Established 1825, Gustavsberg, Sweden; currently in operation

Franz Hagenauer
Born 1906, Austria; trainee at Werkstätte Hagenauer Wien (Hagenauer Workshop, Vienna, see below), 1925; co-managed workshop with brother Karl and sister Grete, beginning 1928; died 1986

Antti Hakkarainen Taidetakomo
Founded in the 1920s, Finland; closed mid-1980s

Suzuki Harunobu
Born Hozumi Jihei, ca. 1724–25, Japan; died 1770, Japan

Howie Glass Co.
Established 1912, Royal Oak, Michigan; currently in operation

International Silver Company
Established 1898, Meriden, Connecticut; hollowware division closed, 1981; flatware division purchased by Syratech Incorporated, East Boston, Massachusetts, 1986; currently in operation

Callie Johnson
Born 1964, Bangor, Maine; CAA student, Department of Design, 1992–94, M.F.A., 1994

Mary Anne Jordan
Born 1957, Toledo, Ohio; CAA student, Department of Fiber, 1983–85, M.F.A., 1985

Wilhelm Kåge
Born 1889, Stockholm, Sweden; designer at A. B. Gustavsberg (see above), 1917–60; art director until 1947; died 1960

Rudolf Knörlein
Born 1902, Vienna, Austria; current status unknown

David Kostich
Born 1967, Akron, Ohio; CAA student, Department of Metalsmithing, 1991–93, M.F.A., 1993

Käthe Kruse Puppen GmbH
Established 1911, Berlin, Germany, by Käthe Kruse (born Katherina Simon, 1833, Breslau, Germany [now Wrocław, Poland]; died 1917, Murnau, Germany); current status unknown

Vicke Lindstrand
Born Viktor Emanuel Lindstrand, 1904, Göteborg, Sweden; designer with Orrefors Glasbruk, 1928–ca. 1940; died 1983, Småland, Sweden

Jussi Mäntynen
Born 1886, Helsinki, Finland; died 1978, Turku, Finland

Lili Markus
Born Erzsi (Elizabeth) Markus, 1888, Hungary; active after 1932

Marianne McCann
Born 1962, Van Nuys, California; CAA student, Department of Fiber, 1987–89, M.F.A., 1989

Michael McCoy
Born 1944, Eaton Rapids, Michigan; CAA department head and artist-in-residence, Department of Design, 1971–95

Brian Meek
Born 1970, Columbus, Ohio; CAA student, Department of Metalsmithing, 1992–94, M.F.A., 1994

Carl Milles
Born 1875, Lagga (near Uppsala), Sweden; CAA department head and artist-in-residence, Department of Sculpture, 1931–51; died 1955, Millesgården, Lidingö, Sweden

Wallace Mitchell
Born 1911, Detroit, Michigan; CAA student, Department of Painting, 1934–35; CAA instructor of drawing and painting, 1936–54; CAA secretary and registrar, 1944–63; CAA museum director, 1955–70; CAA president, 1970–77; died 1977, Bloomfield Hills, Michigan

The Nessen Studio, Inc.
Established 1927 as Nessen Studios, New York City, by Walter von Nessen (born 1889 Iserlohn, Germany; died 1943, New York City); renamed Nessen Lamps, Inc., by 1985; purchased by J. J. I. Lighting Group, Inc., 1987; renamed Nessen Lighting, Inc., ca. 1990; currently in operation

Gerda Nyberg
Employed in the 1930s by Studio Loja Saarinen (see below)

Orrefors Glasbruk
Founded 1726, Småland, Sweden; currently in operation

Pewabic Pottery
Founded 1903, by Mary Chase Perry Stratton with Horace J. Caulkins (born 1850; died 1923), Detroit, Michigan; currently in operation

Charles Phipps
Born 1929, Detroit, Michigan

Charles Phipps and Sons, Ltd.
Established 1949 as Charles Phipps, Inc., Detroit, Michigan, by Charles Phipps (see above); renamed The Old World Shop and relocated in Lexington, Michigan, 1962; renamed Charles Phipps and Sons, Ltd., ca. 1984; currently in operation

M. Christian Friedrich Prange
Born 1756, Germany; active in Halle, Germany; died 1836

Atelier Primavera of Les Grands Magasins du Printemps
Established 1913, Paris, France, by René Guilleré; ceramic objects were made by the Longwy Pottery in Meurthe-et-Moselle and Sainte-Radegonde, France; closed

Reed & Barton Silversmiths
Established as Babbitt & Crossman, 1824, Taunton, Massachusetts; currently in operation

Howard F. Reichenbach
Industrial designer, development engineer, product engineer, and manager, sales and planning, for Chase Brass and Copper Company, Waterbury, Connecticut (see above), ca. 1930s-40s

Eero Saarinen
Born 1910, Kirkkonummi, Finland; student, Yale School of Architecture, 1930-34, B.F.A. 1934; began architectural practice with Eliel Saarinen at Cranbrook, 1936; taught at CAA, 1939-42; married Lilian Swann, 1939; partner, Saarinen, Swanson & Saarinen, 1945-47, Saarinen, Saarinen, and Associates, 1947-50, and Eero Saarinen & Associates, 1950-61; divorced Lilian Swann Saarinen, 1953; married Aline B. Louchheim, 1953; died 1961, Ann Arbor, Michigan

Eliel Saarinen
Born Gottlieb Eliel Saarinen, 1873, Rantasalmi, Finland; partner, Gesellius, Lindgren, Saarinen Architects' Office, 1896-1904; married Mathilda Gyldén, 1899; divorced 1904; married Loja Gesellius (see below), 1904; partner, Gesellius, Saarinen Architects' Office, 1905-1906/7; independent practice, Eliel Saarinen Architects' Office, 1907-23; independent practice, Evanston, Illinois, 1923; visiting professor of architecture, University of Michigan, Ann Arbor, 1923-24; moved to Cranbrook, 1924; independent practice, Cranbrook, beginning 1925; chief architectural advisor, Cranbrook Architectural Office, beginning ca. 1927; partner, Saarinen and Swanson, 1939-44; partner, Saarinen, Swanson & Saarinen, 1945-47; partner, Saarinen, Saarinen, and Associates, 1947-50; resident architect, Cranbrook, 1925-50; CAA president, 1932-46; continued as CAA director of Department of Architecture and Urban Design, 1946-50; died 1950, Saarinen House, Bloomfield Hills, Michigan

Loja Saarinen
Born Louise Gesellius, 1879, Helsinki, Finland; married Eliel Saarinen (see above), 1904; moved to Cranbrook, 1924; directed Studio Loja Saarinen (see below), 1928-42; head, Department of Weaving and Textile Design, 1929-42; moved out of Saarinen House, 1951; died 1968, Bloomfield Hills, Michigan

Laura Sansone
Born 1968, Huntington, New York; CAA student, Department of Fiber, 1992-94, M.F.A., 1994

Helene Sofia Schjerfbeck
Born 1862, Helsinki Finland; died 1946, Saltsjöbaden, Sweden

Viktor Schreckengost
Born 1906, Sebring, Ohio; instructor of design, Cleveland School of Art, 1930-present

Zoltan Sepeshy
Born 1989, Kassa, Hungary (now Kosice, Slovak Republic); CAA faculty, Department of Painting and Drawing, 1931-67; CAA educational director, 1944-46; CAA director, 1946-59; CAA president, 1959-66; died 1974, Royal Oak, Michigan

Greta Skogster-Lehtinen
Born Greta Skogster, 1900, Finland; art director for Kotiahkeruus Oy (Home Industry Co.), 1924-30; operated private studio in Finland, producing textiles, carpets, and tapestries, beginning 1930

Sterling Bronze Company
Established 1901, Brooklyn, New York; closed

Mary Chase Perry Stratton
Born 1867, Hancock, Michigan; co-founded Pewabic Pottery (see above); died 1961, Detroit, Michigan

Studio Loja Saarinen
Established 1928, by Loja Saarinen, Cranbrook, Bloomfield Hills, Michigan; closed 1942

Sunbury Textile Mills, Inc.
Established 1954, Sunbury, Pennsylvania; became a subsidiary of Masco Corporation, Taylor, Michigan (headquarters), 1990; currently in operation

Svenskt Tenn
Located in Stockholm, Sweden, in 1930s; current status unknown

J. Robert F. Swanson
Born 1900, Menominee, Michigan; partner in Swanson and Booth, 1924–26; married Pipsan Saarinen (see below), 1926; operated J. Robert F. Swanson architectural office, 1926–39; partner, Saarinen and Swanson, 1939–44; partner, Saarinen, Swanson & Saarinen, 1945–47; established Swanson Associates, 1947–54, later Swanson Associates, Inc., 1954–81; died 1981, Ann Arbor, Michigan

Pipsan Saarinen Swanson
Born Eva Lisa Saarinen, 1905, Kirkkonummi, Finland; married J. Robert F. Swanson, 1926; head of Interior Design Department, J. Robert F. Swanson architectural firm, 1929–39; instructor at CAA, costume design, batik, and technique, 1932–33; taught introductory course in contemporary interior design, 1935; head of interior design at Saarinen and Swanson, 1939–44; designer for Saarinen-Swanson Furniture, 1939–43; head of interior design for Saarinen, Swanson & Saarinen, 1945–47; partner in Swanson Associates, 1947–54; partner in Swanson Associates, Inc., 1954–79; died 1979, Bloomfield Hills, Michigan

Thompson Glass Co.
Established 1929, Detroit, Michigan; moved to Novi, Michigan, 1979; currently in operation

Unika Vaev USA
Unika Vaev established 1871, by Hørsholm Klædefabrik, Denmark; Unika Vaev USA acquired in 1970 by International Contract Furnishings Inc. (established 1962, New York City); currently in operation

Victor F. von Lossberg
Born in Germany; chief designer at Edward F. Caldwell and Company, Inc., beginning 1894 (see above); president of Caldwell and Company, 1914–ca. 1938; died ca. 1940

Mikhail Vrubel
Born Mikhail Aleksandrovich Vrubel, 1856, Omsk, Siberia, Russia; died 1910, St. Petersburg, Russia

Christine Walsh
Born 1956, South Bend, Indiana; senior designer, Collins and Aikman Corporation (see above), Automotive Division, Bloomfield Hills, Michigan, 1991–93

Charles R. Wermuth and Son, Inc.
Established ca. 1900 as Charles R. Wermuth, Fort Wayne, Indiana; reorganized as Charles R. Wermuth and Son, Inc., before 1922; closed 1978

Werkstätte Hagenauer Wien (Hagenauer Workshop, Vienna)
Established 1898, Vienna; closed

Wilcox Silver Plate Company
A division of the International Silver Company (see above)

Wiltshaw & Robinson, Ltd.
Active 1890–1957, Stoke on Trent, England; renamed Carlton Ware, Ltd., 1958; closed ca. 1989

Maja Andersson Wirde
Born 1873, Ramkvilla, Sweden; instructor of weaving, Cranbrook Foundation, 1929–33; taught courses in textile design and weaving at Studio Loja Saarinen (see above), and in weaving and textiles for CAA; instructor at Kingswood School for girls, 1932–33; died 1952, Algutsboda, Småland, Sweden

Russel Wright
Born 1904, Lebanon, Ohio; died 1976, Lebanon, Ohio

Russel Wright Accessories
Established as Russel Wright Incorporated, 1930, Lebanon, Ohio; renamed Russel Wright Accessories, 1935; later renamed Russel Wright Associates; closed 1967

Ypsilanti Reed Furniture Company, Inc.
Incorporated 1900, Ypsilanti, Michigan; moved to Ionia, Michigan, 1904; renamed Ionia Manufacturing Company and later The Mitchell-Bentley Corporation, ca. 1945; purchased by A. O. Smith, 1964; purchased by General Tire & Rubber Company, 1971; currently in operation

BIBLIOGRAPHY

SELECTED GENERAL BIBLIOGRAPHY

Amberg, Anna-Lisa. *Saarisen Sisustustaide/ Saarinen's Interior Design, 1896–1923.* Helsinki: Taideteollisuusmuseo/Museum of Applied Arts, 1984.

Balmori, Diana. "Cranbrook: The Invisible Landscape." *Journal of the Society of Architectural Historians* 53 (March 1994): 30–60.

Bruegmann, Robert. "When Worlds Collided: European and American Entries to the Chicago Tribune Competition of 1922." In *Chicago Architecture, 1872–1922: Birth of a Metropolis,* ed. John Zukowsky, 302–17. Munich: Prestel-Verlag in association with The Art Institute of Chicago, 1987.

Christ-Janer, Albert, with a foreword by Alvar Aalto. *Eliel Saarinen: Finnish-American Architect and Educator.* 1948. Rev. ed. Chicago: The University of Chicago Press, 1979.

Clark, Robert Judson, et al. *Design in America: The Cranbrook Vision, 1925–1950.* New York: Harry N. Abrams, 1983.

Gerard, John. *Studio Loja Saarinen.* Exhibition catalogue. Bloomfield Hills, Michigan: Cranbrook Academy of Art Museum, 1980.

Hausen, Marika, Kirmo Mikkola, Anna-Lisa Amberg, and Tytti Valto. *Eliel Saarinen: Projects 1896–1923.* Cambridge: The MIT Press, 1990.

The International Competition for a New Administration Building for the Chicago Tribune MCMXXII. Chicago: The Tribune Company, 1923.

The Metropolitan Museum of Art. *The Architect and the Industrial Arts: An Exhibition of Contemporary American Design.* New York: Plandome Press, Inc., for The Metropolitan Museum of Art, 1929.

Pallasmaa, Juhani, ed. *Hvitträsk: Koti Taideteoksena/The Home as a Work of Art.* Helsinki: Otava, 1988.

Pound, Arthur. *The Only Thing Worth Finding: The Life and Legacies of George Gough Booth.* Detroit: Wayne State University Press, 1964.

Pylkkänen, Riitta. *The Use and Traditions of Mediaeval Rugs and Coverlets in Finland.* Helsinki: Suomen Muinaismuistoyhdistys/ Archaeological Society of Finland, 1974.

Rivard, Nancy. "Eliel Saarinen in America." Master's thesis, Wayne State University, Detroit, 1973.

Saarinen, Eliel. *The City: Its Growth, Its Decay, Its Future.* New York: Reinhold, 1943.

Saarinen, Eliel. "A Note on Camillo Sitte." In *The Art of Building Cities: City Building According to its Artistic Fundamentals,* by Camillo Sitte. New York: Reinhold Publishing Corporation, 1945.

Saarinen, Eliel. *The Search for Form in Art and Architecture.* Originally published as *Search for Form: A Fundamental Approach to Art.* New York: Reinhold, 1948. Reprint. New York: Dover, 1985.

Treib, Marc. "Urban Fabric by the Bolt: Eliel Saarinen at Munkkiniemi-Haaga." *Architectural Association Quarterly* 2–3 (1982): 43–58.

Wilk, Christopher. *Frank Lloyd Wright: The Kaufmann Office.* London: The Victoria and Albert Museum, 1993.

Wittkopp, Gregory. "Railway Station and Administrative Building." In *International Dictionary of Architects and Architecture,* ed. Randall J. van Vynckt. Vol. 2, *Architecture:* 170–71.

COMPREHENSIVE BIBLIOGRAPHY, SAARINEN HOUSE, 1930–1950

Bailey, Anson. "The Home of Eliel Saarinen at the Cranbrooke [sic] Academy of Art." *The Master Builder* (August 1934).

"Cranbrook Academy of Art, Bloomfield Hills, Michigan, Eliel Saarinen, Architect." *The Architectural Record* 68 (December 1930): 444–51.

Davies, Florence. "Here, Logic and Beauty are United." *The Detroit News* (September 14, 1930), "Art and Artists" section: 1.

Davies, Florence. "Decorative Arts From Cranbrook Shown at Art Institute." *The Detroit News* (December 20, 1931), "Art and Artists" section: 1.

Fish, Margaret. "Saarinen Cites Keynotes for City's War Memorial." *Milwaukee Sentinel* (ca. February 22, 1947).

Heiden, Margaret. "From the Exhibition of Home Furnishings at Cranbrook." *The Detroit News* (May 12, 1935).

Macomber, Henry P. "The Michigan Home of Eliel Saarinen." *House Beautiful* 64 (October 1933): 133–36.

Reid, Kenneth. "Eliel Saarinen: Master of Design." *Pencil Points* 17 (September 1936): 464–94.

Ryan, Aileen. "Furnish Home According to Principles of Architecture." *The Milwaukee Journal* (January 18, 1942), section 7: 9–10.

SELECTED BIBLIOGRAPHY, SAARINEN HOUSE, 1951-1994

Colby, Joy. "A Living Museum: Cranbrook Restores the Eliel Saarinen Home to its Original Splendor." *The Detroit News* (April 10, 1993).

Gill, Brendan. "Eliel Saarinen at Cranbrook." *Architectural Digest* 50 (April 1993): 28 ff.

Goldberger, Paul. "Bringing Back Saarinen." *The New York Times Magazine* (April 16, 1978): 92 ff.

Mason, Marilynne S. "Cranbrook Academy Revives Eliel Saarinen's House." *The Christian Science Monitor* 85 (September 9, 1993): 10-11.

Miro, Marsha. "The House that Saarinen Built." *Detroit Free Press* (May 15, 1994), section F: 1, 6.

Papademetriou, Peter. "Eliel Saarinen Residence." In *GA/Global Architecture Houses 9*. Tokyo: A.D.A. EDITA Tokyo Co., 1981.

Vallongo, Sally. "Genius of Saarinen family illuminates their house." *The [Toledo] Blade* (June 5, 1994), section H: 1-2.

Wittkopp, Gregory. "Saarinen House dining room restored to original beauty." *Cranbrook Journal* (Fall 1990): 2-3.

Wittkopp, Gregory. "Saarinen House." *Cranbrook Academy of Art Alumni Outline* (Spring 1993): 1-3.

SELECTED PUBLIC MANUSCRIPT COLLECTIONS

Cranbrook Architectural Office Files. Accession number 1989-1. Cranbrook Archives, Cranbrook Educational Community, Bloomfield Hills, Michigan.

Cranbrook Architectural Records. Cranbrook Archives, Cranbrook Educational Community, Bloomfield Hills, Michigan.

George Gough Booth Papers. Accession number 1981-1. Cranbrook Archives, Cranbrook Educational Community, Bloomfield Hills, Michigan.

Saarinen Family Papers. Accession number 1990-08. Cranbrook Archives, Cranbrook Educational Community, Bloomfield Hills, Michigan.

Diana Balmori is principal of Balmori Associates, Landscape & Urban Design, in New Haven, Connecticut, and was responsible for researching the Saarinen House garden and directing the design of its restoration. She teaches at the Yale School of Architecture and the Yale School of Forestry and Environmental Studies. Her most recent publications include *Transitory Gardens, Uprooted Lives* and *Redesigning the American Lawn* (both Yale University Press, 1993).

Patricia Crow joined Balmori Associates in 1991 and was the designer in charge of the Saarinen House garden restoration. She is a graduate of the Rhode Island School of Design and the Landscape Architecture program at Harvard Graduate School of Design. Before joining Balmori Associates she worked in the office of Bruce Kelly/David Varnell in New York City.

Balthazar Korab is an architectural photographer based in Troy, Michigan. He was born in Hungary, trained as an architect in Budapest, and graduated from the École des Beaux-Arts in Paris. He immigrated to the United States in 1955 and joined the firm of Eero Saarinen & Associates in Bloomfield Hills, Michigan, where he pioneered the use of photography in design development. He is the recipient of the prestigious Medal for Architectural Photography, awarded by the American Institute of Architects, and, most recently, he coauthored the *Encyclopedia of American Architecture* (McGraw-Hill, 1994).

David D. J. Rau is Associate Curator at Cranbrook Academy of Art Museum, where his responsibilities include directing the educational programs for Saarinen House. He graduated from the University of Michigan with an M.A. in the History of Art and a Certificate of Museum Practice. Before joining the Cranbrook staff he worked at The Currier Gallery of Art in Manchester, New Hampshire, where he researched the Zimmerman House, designed by Frank Lloyd Wright.

Roy Slade served as President of Cranbrook Academy of Art and Director of Cranbrook Academy of Art Museum from 1977 through 1994. His projects as Director of the Museum included not only initiating and supporting the restoration of Saarinen House, but also guiding the development of the exhibition and catalogue *Design in America: The Cranbrook Vision, 1925-1950* (Abrams, 1983). As the fifth President of the Academy, he lived in Saarinen House until 1991. At that time he established neighboring Milles House as the President's home, which permitted the complete restoration of Saarinen House. Slade moved from his native Wales to the United States to join the Corcoran Gallery and School of Art, Washington, D.C., where he was Dean of the School of Art and Director of the Gallery of Art before he assumed his post at Cranbrook.

Gregory Wittkopp is Director of Cranbrook Academy of Art Museum. In his former position as Curator of Collections for the Museum, he researched and directed the restoration of Saarinen House from 1988 through its transformation into a museum in 1994. He holds a B.S. in Architecture from the College of Architecture and Urban Planning at the University of Michigan and an M.A. in Art History from Wayne State University. He has curated numerous exhibitions and written many essays on the architecture and design of Eliel Saarinen. Before beginning his tenure at Cranbrook he was Curator of Exhibitions at the Saginaw Art Museum, Michigan.

Cranbrook Educational Community is an internationally renowned center for the arts, education, science, and culture located in Bloomfield Hills, Michigan. In addition to Cranbrook Academy of Art and Cranbrook Academy of Art Museum, the community includes Cranbrook Institute of Science, Cranbrook Schools, and other affiliated cultural and educational programs. The Institute of Science is a natural history and science museum serving Michigan and the Great Lakes region. Cranbrook Schools comprise Brookside, an elementary school for students from junior kindergarten through fifth grade, Cranbrook Kingswood Middle School, which offers separate programs for boys and girls in grades six through eight, and Cranbrook Kingswood Upper School, a coeducational day and boarding school for students in grades nine through twelve.

Cranbrook Academy of Art is the country's only school of art solely committed to graduate work. The Academy offers a student body of one hundred forty students from throughout the world a two-year graduate program in nine disciplines: architecture, ceramics, design, fiber, metalsmithing, painting, photography, printmaking, and sculpture. Members of the faculty, usually one to a department, are nationally and internationally renowned artists who live and work at Cranbrook.

Cranbrook Academy of Art Museum is fully accredited by the American Association of Museums. The Cranbrook Collection, the Museum's permanent collection, highlights the achievements of Cranbrook's faculty and students since the community's inception in the 1920s, while the Museum's temporary exhibitions focus on contemporary trends in the visual arts. Since 1994 the museum has operated Saarinen House, offering guided tours from May through October.

PHOTOGRAPH CREDITS

Sandra Ahlers, courtesy Balmori Associates, Inc.: fig. 57; Dick G. Askew, courtesy Cranbrook Archives: figs. 4 (AA-2520), 29 (A of A-2609); Diana Balmori, courtesy Balmori Associates, Inc.: figs. 38, 46, 48; Courtesy Balmori Associates, Inc.: figs. 41, 58; Harvey Croze, courtesy Cranbrook Archives: figs. 15 (2743), 19 (AA-984), 23 (AA-982), 43 (AA-2219-17), 44 (AA-2219-19), 55 (AA-2219-18); Courtesy Cranbrook Academy of Art Museum: figs. 3, 6, 7, 14, 27, 30; Courtesy Cranbrook Archives: figs. 1 (A of A-5169), 2 (CEC-620), 5 (2478), 9 (CEC-816), 11 (CEC-10), 20 (AA-2421-1), 21 (CEC-545), 24 (CEC-623), 25 (AA-617), 28 (A of A-2744), 34 (CEC-1296), 36 (A of A-2757), 37 (CEC-491), 39 (CC-126-1), 40 (5580-3), 42 (CEC-1299), 45 (3693), 47 (CEC-1311), 49 (CEC-549), 50 (CEC-1300), 52 (3691), 53 (AA-993); Habrecht, courtesy Cranbrook Academy of Art Museum: fig. 35; Habrecht, courtesy Cranbrook Archives: figs. 10 (CEC-845), 22 (4550), 31 (AA-2421-3), 32 (AA-2421-4), 33 (AA-2421-5); J. W. Hughes, courtesy Cranbrook Archives: figs. 8 (AA-2421-2), 18 (CEC-1188); Courtesy The Metropolitan Museum of Art, New York: fig. 16 (L11268B); B. G. Miller, courtesy Cranbrook Archives: fig. 12 (AA-2421-6); Frank J. Scherschel, courtesy Cranbrook Archives: fig. 17 (CEC-490); Collection Ronald Saarinen Swanson, courtesy Cranbrook Academy of Art Museum: figs. 13, 51; Betty Truxell, courtesy Cranbrook Archives: fig. 26 (CEC-1220); Lee A. White, courtesy Cranbrook Archives: figs. 54 (CEC-1314), 56 (CEC-1313).

INDEX

Italic page numbers denote illustrations.